REMEMBERING THE CRUCIFIXION

A COLLECTION OF GOOD FRIDAY SERVICES

George A Bowers, Sr.

Copyright © 2022 by George A Bowers, Sr.,
All Rights reserved.

Remembering The Crucifixion
A Collection of Good Friday Services
By George A Bowers, Sr.

ISBN # 978-1-71693-789-7

DEDICATION

This book of Good Friday Services is written for the Glory of God and the praise of His Son, Jesus Christ and is dedicated to my Lord Jesus Christ. Good Friday is the annual remembrance of the greatest love ever given. When Jesus made the ultimate sacrifice for us, it was all because of God's infinite love for us. Nothing we could ever do would honor Him in a way that commemorates this day in the way in which He fully deserves. Nevertheless, because Jesus demands our best and our all, this book of remembrance services is dedicated entirely to Him.

Special thanks to my dear wife, Nancy for her encouragement and prayers and who provided the piano music for most of these services. Thanks also to her mother, Shirley Blozzon, for proofreading the final edition.

Contents

Preface	7
Good Friday Suggestions	8
What Was He Thinking?	11
Colors Of The Cross	27
Sponges	41
Jesus' Cup	61
Beneath The Cross Of Jesus	73
Isaiah and Jesus	85
Afterword	101

Preface

Why A Good Friday Service?

It has always seemed cheap to me to celebrate the joy of Jesus' resurrection on Easter Sunday without pausing to remember His sorrow, suffering, and death a few days before. As worship leaders, we owe it to our congregants to enter into this passion with Jesus and imagine the grief that He and His followers endured that night and following day.

Good Friday services are some of the most special and meaningful services of the year. Unlike most other worship services that are generally celebratory and exciting, this one is very quiet and reflective. In many ways it is similar to a funeral service, in this case, for Jesus Himself. Although He was denied this respect on that first Good Friday, we have the privilege to create one for Him each year on the anniversary of His death.

While the theme of Christ's suffering and crucifixion never changes, there are many possible variations on that theme and this book provides suggestions. Worship leaders are encouraged to adapt rather than adopt. Adapt these services to your own congregation, skills, and setting. Change as appropriate to enable congregants to enter into the crucifixion experience and to "see" it as much as possible. If we have done our job effectively, they should leave in tears as they reflect on the ultimate price Jesus paid for them. I've often been moved to tears myself while conducting this service.

The depths of their (and our) grief will then enable them (and us) to more fully celebrate the truth of Jesus' resurrection on Sunday morning. May God bless you as you serve Him.

Good Friday Suggestions:

This book is a collection of Good Friday Services. Each of these was originally celebrated at the Antioch Church of the Brethren on various dates. Obviously Good Friday is the day on which Jesus was tortured and then crucified. It is always the Friday before Easter and a special time to reflect on the true meaning and deep purpose of Jesus' death.

Here are several general suggestions about conducting a Good Friday service.

1. Whereas other worship services are celebratory, bright, and exciting, by nature, Good Friday Services are quiet, subdued, hushed, and reflective. Try to communicate this mood to your congregants beforehand so that they know what to expect and to come prepared.
2. Keep the focus on Jesus. No symbol or theme should ever overshadow the precious Savior, no matter how compelling. Always be sure He is the center.
3. If possible, dim the lights in the sanctuary or other venue.
4. If available use pianist or organist. If not, recorded music can be used.
5. Full permission is granted to make copies and/or adaptions of the services in this book. That's exactly what it is written for.
6. Most Scripture references are from the New International Version. If another version is preferred, substitution would be easy.
7. I generally like to include as many Deacons and Laypeople in Good Friday Services whenever possible both in reading the Scriptures as well as in prayer and readings. Blanks are provided for people's names who can be assigned. Choose individuals that have strong, loud, and clear voices so that they may be heard. It's best to line these folks up ahead of time so that they know what is expected of them. If worse comes to worst, the pastor can actually do it all him or herself.
8. When laypeople are involved, I've found it helpful to preprint Scriptures and hand out to the various readers. This prevents someone from finding and reading the wrong passage as well as reading it from a paraphrase that may not be accurate. On the other hand, if your laypeople are well versed in the Scripture and have dependable translations, this may not be necessary.
9. Various hymns are suggested in each service. Some of these may not be in the hymn book that your particular congregation uses. Be sure to take the time beforehand not only to check this but also to record the page numbers so they can be announced accurately. I've also found it helpful to have an able vocalist to lead the hymns in a subdued mood and volume. Songs should be chosen that center on the cross. Most hymnals include a section of songs that are appropriate and some songs can be played from CDs or other means as appropriate. Care should be taken to follow all copyright laws and recognize the musicians appropriately.
10. Some of the Good Friday services include suggestions for slides in a PowerPoint. These are not necessary but can be helpful to provide a focus for participants to meditate on. The images for the slides can be found by searching on the internet for royalty free Clipart Images of whatever is suggested. In addition, words to all songs

can be put on the PowerPoint to help participants continue to worship without fooling with hymnals.
11. I have included suggestions for Easter Sunday morning that could continue the Good Friday Service theme if so desired.
12. It is good to give a general reminder like the following at the beginning of each Good Friday Service. This will help to set the tone and provide much needed reminders. It is best to share this as soon as everyone is gathered before anything else begins.

"As we prepare to remember our Lord's death this evening, I encourage each of you to do so reverently and quietly. Please be sure all cell phones and all other electronics are off that we might focus our whole selves on Jesus. Please remind your children if necessary of the reverence and holiness of this service and help them to draw near to Him during this time also. The Psalmist tells us to "Be still and know that I am God." Let us share this special time in His presence quietly as we think about the great sacrifice that Christ made for us."

What Was He Thinking?

(Originally celebrated at Antioch Church of the Brethren on Good Friday 2010)

This Good Friday explores what might have been going through Jesus' mind as He experienced His last few hours.

Tonight as we gather, I would begin with the words to a hymn written by the blind poet, Fanny Crosby:

> Near the Cross, Oh, Lamb of God
> Bring it scenes before me;
> Help me walk from day to day,
> With its shadow o'er me.
> In the cross, In the Cross,
> Be my glory ever,
> Till my raptured soul shall find
> Rest beyond the river.

Tonight we will invite God to bring the scenes of the Cross before us that we might remember once again the awful price that He paid there for our souls.

Selah is a Hebrew word used in the Psalms after certain lines of the text which means to think about that. Stop and ponder on it. Tonight we stop at the cross to ponder on it. To think on it. And to let our ponderings well up into love and gratitude to our Savior.

This service tonight is not a teaching service like Sunday School or Bible Study. It's not for fellowship and socialization. It's not even for preaching and admonition. It is for meditation and reflection. Let's share in singing Verses 2-3 of Beneath The Cross of Jesus.

_____ Beneath the Cross of Jesus Verses 2-3

We will begin tonight after the Last Supper and with Jesus' prayer recorded for us in John 17. We have to wonder tonight what was going through Jesus' mind at some points that night and the next day, but about this, we have no doubt. Jesus made it very plain as He prayed that night. Let's listen in as He speaks to His Father in John 17.

Reader: _____

17:1 "Father, the time has come. Glorify your Son, that your Son may glorify you. 2 For you granted him authority over all people that he might give eternal life to all those you have given him. 3 Now this is eternal life: that they may know you, the only true God, and Jesus Christ, whom you have sent. 4 I have brought you glory on earth by completing the work you gave me to do. 5 And now, Father, glorify me in your presence with the glory I had with you before the world began.
6 "I have revealed you to those whom you gave me out of the world. They were yours; you gave them to me and they have obeyed your word. 7 Now they know that everything you have given me comes from you. 8 For I gave them the words you gave me and they accepted them. They knew with certainty that I came from you, and they believed that you sent me. 9 I pray for them. I am not praying for the world, but for those you have given me, for they are yours. 10 All I have is yours, and all you have is

mine. And glory has come to me through them. 11 I will remain in the world no longer, but they are still in the world, and I am coming to you. Holy Father, protect them by the power of your name-the name you gave me-so that they may be one as we are one. 12 While I was with them, I protected them and kept them safe by that name you gave me. None has been lost except the one doomed to destruction so that Scripture would be fulfilled.

13 "I am coming to you now, but I say these things while I am still in the world, so that they may have the full measure of my joy within them. 14 I have given them your word and the world has hated them, for they are not of the world any more than I am of the world. 15 My prayer is not that you take them out of the world but that you protect them from the evil one. 16 They are not of the world, even as I am not of it. 17 Sanctify them by the truth; your word is truth. 18 As you sent me into the world, I have sent them into the world. 19 For them I sanctify myself, that they too may be truly sanctified.

20 "My prayer is not for them alone. I pray also for those who will believe in me through their message, 21 that all of them may be one, Father, just as you are in me and I am in you. May they also be in us so that the world may believe that you have sent me. 22 I have given them the glory that you gave me, that they may be one as we are one: 23 I in them and you in me. May they be brought to complete unity to let the world know that you sent me and have loved them even as you have loved me.

24 "Father, I want those you have given me to be with me where I am, and to see my glory, the glory you have given me because you loved me before the creation of the world.

25 "Righteous Father, though the world does not know you, I know you, and they know that you have sent me. 26 I have made you known to them, and will continue to make you known in order that the love you have for me may be in them and that I myself may be in them."

What an incredible prayer Jesus prayed that night. Not for sore backs and aching stomachs, but for our courage. For our protection from the evil one. For our unity. For our peace. Imagine going to pray with someone who is on the verge of death and as you take their hand, before you can begin to pray, he or she begins to pray for you instead. That's what Jesus was doing that night. Even as He stared death in the face. Even as He carried the weight of the world's sin, He prayed for you and me. Oh what wondrous Love. Take one finger and hold it up tonight to remind yourself of the prayer Jesus' prayed for the unity of His Church, that we may be one as He and His Father are. And let us pray for the same thing just now silently.

Silent prayer.

Luke 22:39-46 also talks about Jesus praying. Let's listen in once again to His prayer:

Reader: _____

39 Jesus went out as usual to the Mount of Olives, and his disciples followed him. 40 On reaching the place, he said to them, "Pray that you will not fall into temptation." 41

He withdrew about a stone's throw beyond them, knelt down and prayed, 42 "Father, if you are willing, take this cup from me; yet not my will, but yours be done." 43 An angel from heaven appeared to him and strengthened him. 44 And being in anguish, he prayed more earnestly, and his sweat was like drops of blood falling to the ground.
45 When he rose from prayer and went back to the disciples, he found them asleep, exhausted from sorrow. 46 "Why are you sleeping?" he asked them. "Get up and pray so that you will not fall into temptation."

We see in this passage of Scripture the intensity with which Jesus was feeling His own rapidly approaching death. He was beginning to feel the weight of the millstone of our sin come down upon Him.

Have you ever felt guilty for something you have done? Have you ever felt guilty for something someone else did? Perhaps a child or parent or spouse? Jesus was feeling guilty that night. He was feeling all of the guilt from all time. All of the rapes and the molestations. All of the abuses and the slanderings. All of the pride and the arrogance. All of the idolatries and all of our misplaced priorities. All of our missed opportunities. All of the hatred and brutalities of mankind from Adam down to this very moment.

Is it any wonder that His sweat was like great drops of blood? Remember the times you back talked your mom or dad? Jesus was feeling that. The time you lied to your teacher? The time you lied to your boss. The time you lied to your spouse. The time you lied to yourself. He was feeling it all. Satan had offered Him a way to avoid all of this excruciating pain a few years before by just falling and worshipping him. But it was not to be done that way.

One of the things that also hurt Jesus that night was that none of His disciples seemed to care. Their bellies and their drowsiness had gotten the better of them, and not having any caffeine, they were slouching in slumber at the hour of His greatest need.

I wonder tonight how often we've been guilty of that as well. O Lord please forgive us for failing to watch and for failing to pray that we might not fall into temptation. Indeed our spirits are willing, but our bodies are weak. Spend some moments in silent prayer thanking Him for bearing your load that night and for praying for you.

Silent Prayer

He was bearing incredible, excruciating weight and how let down He must have felt during such intense anguish and prayer to find His disciples, His trainees, His best friends, asleep during His time of greatest need. Except for one. One of them wasn't asleep at all. If only he were.

Reader:
47 While he was still speaking a crowd came up, and the man who was called Judas, one of the Twelve, was leading them. He approached Jesus to kiss him, but Jesus asked him, "Judas, are you betraying the Son of Man with a kiss?"

We don't know what all went through Jesus' mind that night. We have little snippets here and there of what He said, but what was He really thinking and feeling? What was he thinking and feeling when one of His closest friends from the past three years betrayed Him with a kiss? Yes, He knew it ahead of time, but that doesn't keep it from hurting. Jesus had invested time and energy and prayer and teaching and love into this man who held so much potential. And now, for filthy money or for political popularity or for whatever other reasons, he betrayed the King of Glory into the hands of those who would torture and kill Him.

I know what I'd be feeling, Anger and Resentment. Fight or Flight. And yet, we see Jesus doing none of these. From what we know of Jesus, my guess is that He was feeling compassion toward Judas knowing what agony this action would cost Him. Knowing that it didn't have to be that way. Knowing that they both would suffer for this betrayal.

And with a kiss of all things. A kiss is a symbol of affection. Over and over again in the New Testament we are commanded to greet each other with a holy kiss. And yet, Judas greeted our Lord with a most unholy kiss of betrayal. I pray that our affections toward the Savior are not for personal gain. Not for personal advancement at Christ's expense. But that they would be true expressions of our deep love for Him. Give your Savior a true kiss of adoration and love tonight.

John's gospel tells us that the angry mob that came to arrest Jesus that dark night were carrying torches and lanterns. And I wonder if Jesus was remembering when He had first created Light. Remembering that He Himself was the Light. Remembering the Unapproachable Light in which He lived in in Glory with the Father. Remembering also the flames of hell which would one day likely consume those now carrying the torches, and those who would drive the nails, and crack the whips. "Father forgive," He later prayed for all of these, "for they know not what they do."

He must have been thinking something about this contrast between Light and Darkness. About the spiritual battle now being waged in the heavenly realms. For verses 49-53 tell us:

Reader:
49 When Jesus' followers saw what was going to happen, they said, "Lord, should we strike with our swords?" 50 And one of them struck the servant of the high priest, cutting off his right ear.

51 But Jesus answered, "No more of this!" And he touched the man's ear and healed him.
52 Then Jesus said to the chief priests, the officers of the temple guard, and the elders, who had come for him, "Am I leading a rebellion, that you have come with swords and clubs? 53 Every day I was with you in the temple courts, and you did not lay a hand on me. But this is your hour-when darkness reigns."

Touch your ear tonight to remind yourself of the incredible grace and forgiveness of Jesus Christ in healing His enemy's ear. Even up to the very end, Jesus was healing. He was loving. He was teaching. And He was thinking. Thinking about the hour when darkness would reign. We sometimes refer to a period of history called the Dark Ages, but the world has never been darker than what it was over that Thursday night, Good Friday, and Saturday when the Light of the World had been snuffed out on the cross.

Reader:
54 Then seizing him, they led him away.

I wonder what Jesus thought about the iron shackles they likely used to hold Him. Was He thinking of that day of Creation when He designed the iron molecule? Was He thinking of how foolish it was that they thought they could hold the Creator with something he had created?

Was He thinking of the chains of iron that held the souls of these men imprisoned. Chains of hatred and bitterness. Greed and pride. Fear and harshness. Was He thinking of the words of the Psalmist that declares in 107:16

Reader:
16 The Lord breaks down gates of bronze and cuts through bars of iron.

No, It wasn't the iron that held Him. It was His love for us and His steadfast obedience to the will of His Father in order to save all mankind who would accept that salvation.

Reader:
54 They took him into the house of the high priest.

I wonder what He thought when He entered the house of Caiaphas, the High Priest. The Great Eternal High Priest of Heaven Himself was at the house of the temporal high priest in Jerusalem. I wonder if Jesus was thinking about Melchizedek, the king of Salem whom Abraham met with. Was He thinking about when He and the Father first appointed Aaron and his sons to the priesthood in the desert some 1500 years earlier? And how far it had fallen. How corrupt it had become. Was He thinking about the ultimate blood sacrifice He Himself would make in just a few hours and about how He would carry that blood into Heaven's Holy of Holies? I can hear Him echoing the words He said just outside the city a few days earlier, would that you knew the things that make for peace.

Reader:
63-64 The men who were guarding Jesus began mocking and beating him. They blindfolded him and demanded, "Prophesy! Who hit you?"

I wonder what He thought when they did this? "Prophecy who hit me? I can tell you the number of hairs on your head, what you did every second of every day last year, and where you'll be in a thousand years. I can tell everyone about that ugly mole on your back and about what you did when you thought no one was looking." Like He did with the woman at the well, He could've told all, but He didn't. He silently took the abuse for you and me.

Reader:
65 And they said many other insulting things to him.

Imagine the insulting things they must have said to the King of Glory. Things about His earthly mother and father. Things about His God. Things about His people the Jews. Things about His looks, about His body. Things others have probably all said about us and perhaps we've said about others. Not **some** insulting things, but many. Mark describes it this way: 15:17-20

Reader:
17 They put a purple robe on him, then twisted together a crown of thorns and set it on him. 18 And they began to call out to him, "Hail, king of the Jews!" 19 Again and again they struck him on the head with a staff and spit on him. Falling on their knees, they paid homage to him. 20 And when they had mocked him, they took off the purple robe and put his own clothes on him. Then they led him out to crucify him.

I wonder if Jesus was thinking about the violet stripe in the rainbow He'd made for all of us about 2500 years earlier? Of the promise He'd made with these people not to destroy them again with water for their abject wickedness? Was He thinking of the blue and scarlet cloths laid over the showbread as it was about to be moved from one place to another as He, the Living Bread was about to be moved? Was He thinking about His Royal Seat in the ages to come?

And what did He think of that crown of thorns? Was He remembering the time when thorns first appeared on the earth recorded for us in Gen 3:17-18

Reader:
17 To Adam he said, "Because you listened to your wife and ate from the tree about which I commanded you, 'You must not eat of it,' "Cursed is the ground because of you; through painful toil you will eat of it all the days of your life.
18 It will produce thorns and thistles for you, and you will eat the plants of the field.

Was He thinking to Himself, "I'm dying to take these very thorns away? The ones brought about by your ancestor's disobedience!!" If you have a fingernail, take it and press it into your scalp. Not hard enough to bring the blood, but hard enough to hurt. And let it remind you of what Jesus felt that night.

When they spit upon Him, was He thinking of Job who said, Job 17:1-6; 30:9-10

Reader: _____

1 My spirit is broken, my days are cut short, the grave awaits me.
2 Surely mockers surround me; my eyes must dwell on their hostility.
3 "Give me, O God, the pledge you demand. Who else will put up security for me?
4 You have closed their minds to understanding; therefore you will not let them triumph.
5 If a man denounces his friends for reward, the eyes of his children will fail.
6 "God has made me a byword to everyone, a man in whose face people spit.
9 "And now their sons mock me in song; I have become a byword among them.
10 They detest me and keep their distance; they do not hesitate to spit in my face.

Was He remembering the time He healed the blind man with His own saliva. Was He thinking of God's promise to spit out of His mouth all those who are lukewarm? It's not very sanitary, I know, but lick your finger and wipe it on your own cheek to remind you of the sinners' spit running down Jesus' face. That was far less sanitary.

Oh what a horrible picture of humanity. Of us. Abusing the very God that became flesh. The God that showed us love. The God that heals us. The Creator that voluntarily submitted to His Creation in order to save it. Being mocked, and beaten, and spit upon, and abused by His created beings.

_____ At the Cross Verses 1-3

After this first abuse, Jesus was tried before the Jewish leaders, the Sanhedrin, which was the Jewish Supreme Court. He was tried before Pilate. He was tried before Herod. And He was taken back to Pilate. We don't know what was going through His mind as He stood in all these courtrooms. But I can imagine once or twice His mind considered His own Courtroom in Heaven and the time when Pilate and Herod and each member of the Sanhedrin would have to one day stand before His judgment seat. Did He think of the list of charges against these that sat judging Him?

The hours were going by-up all night, anguish, pain, suffering. It was now either early or mid-morning when we read from John 19:4-5

Reader: _____

Once more Pilate came out and said to the Jews, "Look, I am bringing him out to you to let you know that I find no basis for a charge against him." 5 When Jesus came out wearing the crown of thorns and the purple robe, Pilate said to them, "Here is the man!"

What Pilate said in Greek when He stated, "Here is the Man" was actually more like, "Look at this poor guy. He's weak and mutilated and bleeding. Don't you think this is enough?" Pilate really wanted to do the right thing initially, he just didn't have the wherewithal to pull it off. So much like us. Without the Holy Spirit, our good intentions end in horrible tragedy.

He thought the horrible sight in front of them would arouse their pity. It did not. Unfortunately, it incited their rage. When raising young quail, if one starts to bleed in any way, its death is certain unless it can be removed from the pen. The other birds will quickly mob it and peck it until it is dead and lifeless.

The same thing happens on school busses as mobs attack any child who shows signs of weakness. And the same thing happened to Jesus. I wonder what went through His mind as He stood there wounded and bleeding?

From the words of the songwriter, Avis Christiansen,
Father Forgive them, thus did He pray, E'en while His lifeblood, flowed fast away
Praying for sinners while in such woe, No one but Jesus, ever loved so.
Blessed Redeemer, Precious Redeemer! Seems now I see Him on Calvary's tree,
Wounded and Bleeding, for sinners pleading, Blind and unheeding, dying for me.

Today it's likely that most of us in the same situation would be tempted to lash out in whatever weak way we could. Some obscene gesture. Some hateful comment. Jesus did none of that. He stood there quietly loving them and us.

John 19:6-7   Reader: _____

6 As soon as the chief priests and their officials saw him, they shouted, "Crucify! Crucify!" But Pilate answered, "You take him and crucify him. As for me, I find no basis for a charge against him."
7 The Jews insisted, "We have a law, and according to that law he must die, because he claimed to be the Son of God."

When those in power have a goal in mind, we mustn't let justice nor righteousness get in the way. Crucify they shouted. Say Crucify out loud tonight. And crucify they would. I wonder if Jesus thought about the time He had granted each of these humans their first breath of air. When He had breathed into Adam the Breath of Life to begin with. When He had created the tongues that now shouted for His own death. Death to the Author of their Life.

John 19:8-12 Reader: _____

8 When Pilate heard this, he was even more afraid, 9 and he went back inside the palace. "Where do you come from?" he asked Jesus, but Jesus gave him no answer. 10 "Do you refuse to speak to me?" Pilate said. "Don't you realize I have power either to free you or to crucify you?"
11 Jesus answered, "You would have no power over me if it were not given to you from above. Therefore the one who handed me over to you is guilty of a greater sin." 12 From then on, Pilate tried to set Jesus free,

It's interesting to me that Pilate was afraid. He is the one with all the power and the weapons and the soldiers and wealth and Jesus is the weak helpless poor prisoner. Or so it seems. And Pilate is the one afraid! Never in this whole horrible weekend do we see Jesus afraid. Sorrowed yes, disappointed yes, but never once fearful. Pilate of all people is afraid.

And so Pilate talks to Jesus threatening Him with death when He wouldn't answer. To which Jesus replied very calmly and directly, "You would have no power unless it was given to you by God."

And then Pilate became really scared and tried harder than ever to find a way to release Jesus. Imagine this poor spineless, one horse Roman ruler standing before the One who created authority itself. Who created leadership. What lessons Jesus could have taught him. What seminars He could have given on motivation and loyalty and integrity and winning friends and influencing people. But Pilate was in no mood to listen and so it was not to be.

John 19:12 Reader: _____

12 From then on, Pilate tried to set Jesus free, but the Jews kept shouting, "If you let this man go, you are no friend of Caesar. Anyone who claims to be a king opposes Caesar."

God forbid that we ever choose Caesar over Christ! Paul wrestled with this question as he asked in Galatians 1:10 Am I now trying to win the approval of men, or of God?

Indeed, that is a question we all must ask ourselves regularly. Judas had already made his choice that night. He chose to please men. Peter made the same poor choice and thankfully later changed his mind in bitter tears. Pilate also made this choice. When his position of earthly power and wealth and status were threatened, Pilate chose the approval of men, in this case Caesar. We have seen the same scene played out many times over in our own time where a leader perhaps wants to do right, but to keep his or her seat of power or prestige, a compromise is made and a deal is struck. For Pilate, it was very eternally sad. Who will you please in life? God or men?

I want us to notice tonight how Judas's money played a part as well as Pilate's power. No wonder the Bible has such strong warnings for us concerning these very strong forces in our world. Political issues were in play that night as well as financial ones. Religious issues and issues of power. The more things change, the more they stay the same. The Jewish leaders also chose Caesar as the next few verses tell us.

John 19:13-15   Reader: _____

13 When Pilate heard this, he brought Jesus out and sat down on the judge's seat at a place known as the Stone Pavement (which in Aramaic is Gabbatha). 14 It was the day of Preparation of Passover Week, about the sixth hour.
"Here is your king," Pilate said to the Jews.
15 But they shouted, "Take him away! Take him away! Crucify him!"
"Shall I crucify your king?" Pilate asked.
"We have no king but Caesar," the chief priests answered.

I wonder what Jesus thought about His people's response? No king but Caesar? How about David and his royal line? How about all the Old Testament laws against idolatry? Indeed, they signed their own fate as they rejected Jesus in favor of Caesar.

John 19:16   Reader: _____

Finally Pilate handed him over to them to be crucified.

We see here the ultimate cave-in. The ultimate surrender. Another Gospel tells us that Pilate then washed his hands to indicate his innocence. Good luck with that.

I wonder tonight what was going through Jesus' mind as He watched Pilate trying to cleanse himself of his own guilt. What a waste of good water and time.

Was Jesus thinking about where each molecule of that water had been in the last 2000 years. It's exact location in the Great Flood of Noah and how it had cascaded over a place Pilate had never heard of before but would one day be called Niagara Falls. Was He thinking forward to how it would one day be used in the baptism of some future Christians somewhere in the world? Was He thinking of His own blood which could truly wash away Pilate's guilt? Wring your hands as if you are washing them tonight to remind you of Pilate's vain attempt to come clean. All this happened about 6 o'clock in the morning.

John 19:16-24 goes on to tell us then of the preparations that were made for the Crucifixion.

Reader: _____

So the soldiers took charge of Jesus. 17 Carrying his own cross, he went out to the place of the Skull (which in Aramaic is called Golgotha). 18 Here they crucified him, and with him two others-one on each side and Jesus in the middle.
19 Pilate had a notice prepared and fastened to the cross. It read: JESUS OF NAZARETH, THE KING OF THE JEWS. 20 Many of the Jews read this sign, for the place where Jesus was crucified was near the city, and the sign was written in Aramaic,

Latin and Greek. 21 The chief priests of the Jews protested to Pilate, "Do not write 'The King of the Jews,' but that this man claimed to be king of the Jews."
22 Pilate answered, "What I have written, I have written."
23 When the soldiers crucified Jesus, they took his clothes, dividing them into four shares, one for each of them, with the undergarment remaining. This garment was seamless, woven in one piece from top to bottom.
24 "Let's not tear it," they said to one another. "Let's decide by lot who will get it." This happened that the scripture might be fulfilled which said,
"They divided my garments among them and cast lots for my clothing."
So this is what the soldiers did.

Let's sing Verses 1-4 of When I Survey The Wondrous Cross, number _____

    Jesus was crucified about 9am in the morning. I wonder what He thought as He was nailed to that piece of wood that He Himself had created. Was He thinking of the Tree of Life that stood in the Garden that mankind had been prohibited from returning to?

    Was He thinking of the wood He provided that was used in the ark that saved the human race in the Great Flood? Was He thinking of the cedars of Lebanon used for the mighty Temple of God.

    What did He think as those cold metal nails were driven into and through His flesh? Take your finger tonight and press into your wrist and imagine what it would be like for a nail to be hammered through there. Take your finger and press into your ankle and imagine the pain that would cause.

    As Jesus struggled toward Golgotha with His cross, was He thinking about how Abraham had offered up Isaac at this very spot some 1900 years earlier? Was He thinking about how ironic it was that He would be crucified at the Place of the Skull which would symbolize dead humanity? Was He thinking how He had felt when He had sculpted this very hill during Creation knowing what was going to happen here today? Was He thinking of the skulls of millions of people that would come forth from their graves because of what He would accomplish in the next few days? Touch your chin tonight to remind yourself of Golgotha, the place of the Skull upon which Jesus died.

    What did Jesus think of the soldiers on either side? I imagine even then He was praying for their souls, for He carried their sin as well. Whatever it was that brought the sentence they now suffered as well as every other sin in their past and ours. The cross itself only had to hold the 150 pounds or so of Jesus' body. But Jesus had to support the weight of the sins of the world.

    What did He think about Simon of Cyrene who carried His cross for Him part of the way? And did He pray for Simon's sons Alexander and Rufus?

Matthew adds some details that John doesn't record about some of what Jesus endured on the cross.

Matt 27:39-46   Reader: _____

39 Those who passed by hurled insults at him, shaking their heads 40 and saying, "You who are going to destroy the temple and build it in three days, save yourself! Come down from the cross, if you are the Son of God!"
41 In the same way the chief priests, the teachers of the law and the elders mocked him. 42 "He saved others," they said, "but he can't save himself! He's the King of Israel! Let him come down now from the cross, and we will believe in him. 43 He trusts in God. Let God rescue him now if he wants him, for he said, 'I am the Son of God.'" 44 In the same way the robbers who were crucified with him also heaped insults on him.

I wonder what Jesus thought as the priests and the teachers of the law of all people, came by to mock Him. He saved others but He cannot save Himself. Indeed by not saving Himself, by willingly sacrificing Himself up, He was saving others. Many others. Even them, if they would accept Him.

Matthew goes on to tell us that

Reader: _____
45 From the sixth hour until the ninth hour darkness came over all the land.

Was Jesus remembering the longest day? When He had stopped the sun so that Joshua could complete the battle? Today, as darkness surrounded, Jesus was completing His own battle.

Reader: _____
46 About the ninth hour Jesus cried out in a loud voice, "Eloi, Eloi, lama sabachthani?"-which means, "My God, my God, why have you forsaken me?"

While many people have wondered how God could have forsaken Jesus on the cross, we find that He was in reality, quoting one of the Scriptures that spoke so clearly of this event. He was calling all of our attention to what was really happening here by singing the first line of Psalm 22. Let's listen to it all:

Ps 22   Reader: _____
My God, my God, why have you forsaken me? Why are you so far from saving me, so far from the words of my groaning? 2 O my God, I cry out by day, but you do not answer, by night, and am not silent.
3 Yet you are enthroned as the Holy One; you are the praise of Israel. 4 In you our fathers put their trust; they trusted and you delivered them. 5 They cried to you and were saved; in you they trusted and were not disappointed.

6 But I am a worm and not a man, scorned by men and despised by the people. 7 All who see me mock me; they hurl insults, shaking their heads: 8 "He trusts in the LORD; let the LORD rescue him. Let him deliver him, since he delights in him."

9 Yet you brought me out of the womb; you made me trust in you even at my mother's breast. 10 From birth I was cast upon you; from my mother's womb you have been my God. 11 Do not be far from me, for trouble is near and there is no one to help.

12 Many bulls surround me; strong bulls of Bashan encircle me. 13 Roaring lions tearing their prey open their mouths wide against me. 14 I am poured out like water, and all my bones are out of joint. My heart has turned to wax; it has melted away within me. 15 My strength is dried up like a potsherd, and my tongue sticks to the roof of my mouth; you lay me in the dust of death. 16 Dogs have surrounded me, a band of evil men has encircled me, they have pierced my hands and my feet. 17 I can count all my bones; people stare and gloat over me. 18 They divide my garments among them and cast lots for my clothing.

19 But you, O LORD, be not far off; O my Strength, come quickly to help me. 20 Deliver my life from the sword, my precious life from the power of the dogs. 21 Rescue me from the mouth of the lions; save me from the horns of the wild oxen.

22 I will declare your name to my brothers; in the congregation I will praise you. 23 You who fear the LORD, praise him! All you descendants of Jacob, honor him! Revere him, all you descendants of Israel! 24 For he has not despised or disdained the suffering of the afflicted one; he has not hidden his face from him but has listened to his cry for help.

25 From you comes the theme of my praise in the great assembly; before those who fear you will I fulfill my vows. 26 The poor will eat and be satisfied; they who seek the LORD will praise him--may your hearts live forever! 27 All the ends of the earth will remember and turn to the LORD, and all the families of the nations will bow down before him, 28 for dominion belongs to the LORD and he rules over the nations.

29 All the rich of the earth will feast and worship; all who go down to the dust will kneel before him--those who cannot keep themselves alive. 30 Posterity will serve him; future generations will be told about the Lord. 31 They will proclaim his righteousness to a people yet unborn--for he has done it.

Jesus knew Psalm 22 since He had helped David write it 1000 years earlier, showing Him very vividly what would happen on Calvary that day. And so Jesus quoted from it here trying to explain to all those watching exactly what was happening. But since most of them didn't know their Bibles, they tragically missed the connection. Jesus did not, as the next few verses from John tell us.

John 19:28 Reader:
Later, knowing that all was now completed, and so that the Scripture would be fulfilled, Jesus said, "I am thirsty." 29 A jar of wine vinegar was there, so they soaked a sponge in it, put the sponge on a stalk of the hyssop plant, and lifted it to Jesus' lips.

Thirst is one of the chief agonies of death by crucifixion. The loss of blood and the exposure to the elements of the weather generated intense thirst. Swallow hard and think what it's like to be really, really thirsty.

I wonder if Jesus, when He saw the wine vinegar thought of the water He had turned into wine. If He thought of Israel, the vine in His parable planted by God in the richest soil and tended with the best care, only to have it bear no fruit. Was He thinking of the abundant fruit that His obedience would produce?

He was almost certainly thinking of Ps 69:21 which says, "They put gall in my food and gave me vinegar for my thirst."

Reader: _____

30 When he had received the drink, Jesus said, "It is finished." With that, he bowed his head and gave up his spirit.

Jesus knew that all was now completed. He knew it was finished. He knew His earthly work was ended and that the time for the evening sacrifice had come. He Himself would be that evening's sacrifice. Crying out at the same time the lamb did over at the temple altar. Did He think of Abraham's lamb that spared Isaac on this very hillside? Did He remember what His cousin had called Him three years earlier, The Lamb of God that takes away the sin of the world?

And so the sacrifice was made and as Jesus said, "It was finished."

John 19:31   Reader: _____

31 Now it was the day of Preparation, and the next day was to be a special Sabbath. Because the Jews did not want the bodies left on the crosses during the Sabbath, they asked Pilate to have the legs broken and the bodies taken down. 32 The soldiers therefore came and broke the legs of the first man who had been crucified with Jesus, and then those of the other. 33 But when they came to Jesus and found that he was already dead, they did not break his legs. 34 Instead, one of the soldiers pierced Jesus' side with a spear, bringing a sudden flow of blood and water. 35 The man who saw it has given testimony, and his testimony is true. He knows that he tells the truth, and he testifies so that you also may believe. 36 These things happened so that the scripture would be fulfilled: "Not one of his bones will be broken,"   37 and, as another scripture says, "They will look on the one they have pierced."

Let's sing number _____ The Old Rugged Cross verses 1-4

Reader: _____

38 Later, Joseph of Arimathea asked Pilate for the body of Jesus. Now Joseph was a disciple of Jesus, but secretly because he feared the Jews. With Pilate's permission, he came and took the body away. 39 He was accompanied by Nicodemus, the man who earlier had visited Jesus at night. Nicodemus brought a mixture of myrrh and aloes,

about seventy-five pounds. 40 Taking Jesus' body, the two of them wrapped it, with the spices, in strips of linen. This was in accordance with Jewish burial customs. 41 At the place where Jesus was crucified, there was a garden, and in the garden a new tomb, in which no one had ever been laid. 42 Because it was the Jewish day of Preparation and since the tomb was nearby, they laid Jesus there.

And there we shall leave Him until we return with the women on Sunday morning.

Let's Close by singing _____ Were You There? Verses 1-3

As we think about the painful crucifixion of our Lord tonight, may we rededicate ourselves to Him, determined to love as He loved, to suffer if need be as He suffered. And to be ever true and faithful to Him.

Closing Prayer of Thanksgiving.

Suggestion for Easter Sunday: What was Jesus thinking during the resurrection? What was He thinking about the women who came and the disciples who didn't believe them?

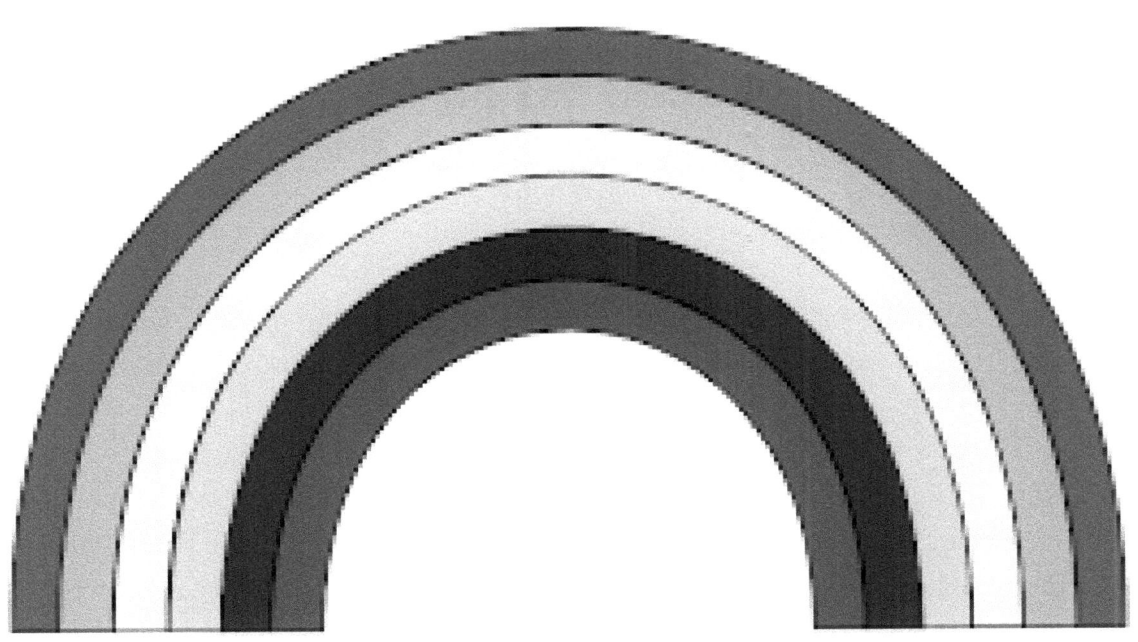

Colors Of The Cross

(Originally celebrated at Antioch Church of the Brethren on Good Friday 2014)

This Good Friday Service walks through the events of
Good Friday using many different common colors.

In order to help congregants enter this experience, prepare a pack of papers
for each person beforehand. This can be done by cutting colored
construction paper into four equal pieces in the following order:
Brown, Black, Orange, Purple, Yellow, White, Red, Green
Provide a small square of aluminum foil as well.

It's also helpful to prepare a PowerPoint that also has slides of
these colors in the same order as well as others as indicated.

Slide 1 Jesus on the Cross

Leader

Please check to be sure all cell phones are silenced during our time of remembrance and reflection this evening. Does everyone have papers? You will need to go through your stack to find the right colors as we go along.

Opening Prayer

This is in many ways, a memorial service for Jesus Christ. At a memorial, it is a common custom to read an obituary of the recently departed. Let me share that with you now. **Slide 1 (Jesus on the Cross)**

Jesus, 33, of the last known address of Nazareth, died Friday on Mount Calvary just outside Jerusalem. The area is also known as Golgotha, or Skull Hill. Betrayed by one of His own disciples, Jesus was crucified on order of the Roman Governor Pontius Pilate. The causes of death were extreme exhaustion, severe torture, and loss of blood.

Jesus was born in a stable in Bethlehem around the year 0 AD and was a descendent of Abraham, Judah, and David and was the son of His devoted mother, Mary also of Nazareth. He was predeceased by His earthly father, Joseph and He is survived by a number of brothers and sisters, 11 disciples, and numerous other followers.

He was self-educated and spent the last three years of His life working as a Teacher. He also occasionally worked as a medical doctor and it is reported that he healed many patients of everything from blindness to leprosy. Up until the time of His Death, Jesus was teaching and sharing good news, healing the sick, touching the lonely, feeding the hungry and helping the poor.

Jesus was most noted for telling parables about His Father's Kingdom and performing miracles such as feeding over 5,000 people with only five loaves and two fish. His body was quickly buried in a stone grave donated by Joseph of Arimethea, a loyal friend and follower. By order of Pilate, a boulder has been rolled in front of the tomb and it is now sealed with several Roman guards on patrol. In lieu of flowers, the family has requested that everyone try to live as Jesus did. Donations may be sent to anyone in need.

Let us honor and remember this Great God-Man this evening.

Please turn to Hymn _____ and let us sing Beneath the Cross of Jesus verses 1-2

During this time of early Spring, it is so wonderful to look around and see all the beautiful colors. This evening we want to consider the various colors of the crucifixion, some pretty, some not so much.

At our last Communion Service, we shared a special time together around the Lord's Table remembering the last supper that Jesus shared with His disciples in Jerusalem so many years ago. Tonight we pick up shortly thereafter from Mark 14.

Slide 2 (Jesus praying in Gethsemane)

Co-Leader _____
32 They went to a place called Gethsemane, and Jesus said to his disciples, "Sit here while I pray." 33 He took Peter, James and John along with him, and he began to be deeply distressed and troubled. 34 "My soul is overwhelmed with sorrow to the point of death," he said to them. "Stay here and keep watch."

Leader
What color is agony? What color is loneliness and grief? Perhaps the black of Gethsemane's ripe olives represents the color that was in Jesus' soul that night. **Slide 3 (Black).** (Find your black sheet). Even as the olives of Gethsemane turn dark as they ripen, so now as His ministry was nearing its fulfillment, the black began to close in. The weight of the sins of billions of people was beginning to press upon His holy shoulders. The pain of His heart being torn away from the Father's love for the first and only time in all eternity.

"My soul is overwhelmed with sorrow to the point of death." Those are mighty painful words from the strongest Man who ever lived. It's hard to imagine Jesus being overwhelmed with anything, much less sorrow, and yet these are His words that night. Have you ever felt grief and sadness so deeply that you thought it would literally kill you? Jesus was there that night. In fact, Luke says that His anguish was so great that His sweat was like drops of blood. **Slide 4 (Jesus praying in Gethsemane)**

Mark continues: Co-Leader _____
35 Going a little farther, he fell to the ground and prayed that if possible the hour might pass from him. 36 "Abba, Father," he said, "everything is possible for you. Take this cup from me. Yet not what I will, but what you will."

Leader:

He fell to the ground and prayed for another way. Any other way. All things are possible with God and He had seen His Father do the impossible many times. Wasn't there some other way now? Any other way, besides drinking this black cup of suffering and agony?

And then setting the example for all who will follow Him, He says submissively, "Yet not what I will, but what you will. If this is what You know needs to happen, I'll do it. I'll endure it. I'll suffer it. If this is the path you have chosen for Me to tread, I'll walk it. Regardless of the pain and cost, regardless of whether I understand Your purposes or not, I'll drink this cup." Even in His last hours, Jesus was still teaching and setting an example for us all.

But He was hurting. And so He reached out to His closest disciples, Peter, James and John to help Him in His hour of greatest need. He needed companionship as He groped through the blackness of dark Gethsemane. "Stay here and keep watch," He asked. This was one of the few times He asked anything personally of His disciples, but unfortunately, they did not deliver. Instead of bright rays of hope, they would only bring Him more black sorrow that night.

Co-Leader _____

37 Then he returned to his disciples and found them sleeping. "Simon," he said to Peter, "are you asleep? Could you not keep watch for one hour? 38 Watch and pray so that you will not fall into temptation. The spirit is willing, but the body is weak."
39 Once more he went away and prayed the same thing. 40 When he came back, he again found them sleeping, because their eyes were heavy. They did not know what to say to him.

Leader:

The spirit is willing, but the flesh is weak. And whenever we allow the flesh to control us, we too will disappoint the Savior. The abandonment He felt from those who were His closest earthly friends only compounded His grief.

Let's sing Beneath the Cross _____ verses 3-4

Co-Leader _____

The disciples would not sleep for long for shortly thereafter, Mark records these words: Mark 14 **Slide 5 (Jesus being arrested in the Garden).**

41 Returning the third time, he said to them, "Are you still sleeping and resting? Enough! The hour has come. Look, the Son of Man is betrayed into the hands of sinners. 42 Rise! Let us go! Here comes my betrayer!"

43 Just as he was speaking, Judas, one of the Twelve, appeared. With him was a crowd armed with swords and clubs, sent from the chief priests, the teachers of the law, and the elders.

44 Now the betrayer had arranged a signal with them: "The one I kiss is the man; arrest him and lead him away under guard." 45 Going at once to Jesus, Judas said, "Rabbi!" and kissed him. 46 The men seized Jesus and arrested him. 47 Then one of those standing near drew his sword and struck the servant of the high priest, cutting off his ear.

48 "Am I leading a rebellion," said Jesus, "that you have come out with swords and clubs to capture me? 49 Every day I was with you, teaching in the temple courts, and you did not arrest me. But the Scriptures must be fulfilled." 50 Then everyone deserted him and fled.

Leader:

What color do you paint a traitor? One whom you trusted and then he turns on you? What color do you paint deserters? Ones whom you wished would stand with you but who ran when the fear became too great. **Slide 6 (Yellow)** Perhaps yellow is the best color for that. (Find your yellow sheet). Yellow is often the color of cowardice. After just a little while earlier promising their undying allegiance, every one of them deserted Jesus that night and fled. Their bold courage shifted suddenly to yellow when their own necks were threatened.

As we celebrate Easter and behold the daffodils, let us not forget the yellow disciples who left Jesus alone during His darkest hour. And let us pray for the courage to never do the same, but to follow through with our commitments.

Co-Leader _____
Luke 22:54-62 **Slide 7 (Peter betraying Jesus)**

54 Then seizing him, they led him away and took him into the house of the high priest. Peter followed at a distance. 55 But when they had kindled a fire in the middle of the courtyard and had sat down together, Peter sat down with them. 56 A servant girl saw him seated there in the firelight. She looked closely at him and said, "This man was with him."

57 But he denied it. "Woman, I don't know him," he said.

58 A little later someone else saw him and said, "You also are one of them."

"Man, I am not!" Peter replied.

59 About an hour later another asserted, "Certainly this fellow was with him, for he is a Galilean."

60 Peter replied, "Man, I don't know what you're talking about!" Just as he was speaking, the rooster crowed. 61 The Lord turned and looked straight at Peter. Then Peter remembered the word the Lord had spoken to him: "Before the rooster crows today, you will disown me three times." 62 And he went outside and wept bitterly.

Leader:

The blackness of the night was chased away with the orange flames of a fire. **Slide 8. (Orange)** We can smell the smoke as it ascended from the crackling wood. The flickering orange light would be enough for one of those standing close by to correctly identify Peter as a follower of Jesus. After running at the moment of arrest, he evidently snuck along behind in the shadows wanting to keep close enough to find out what was going to happen to Jesus. And because he got cold, before he knew it he found himself warming himself beside the fire of the high priest. While his body grew warmer from the fire, his heart was growing colder.

Peter was recognized by three different people around that fire pit that night. And each time he was questioned about it, his answers progressively got worse. "I don't know Jesus. I have nothing to do with Him. I don't even know what you're talking about." And as soon as he spoke the last of his denials, the rooster knew it was time to wake up Jerusalem. And as he did so, Peter woke up too and realized what he had done. And he wept bitterly. Let us be careful whose fire we warm ourselves beside. **Slide 9 (Peter betraying Jesus smaller with Orange outline)**

Perhaps the orange fire reminded Peter of hell fire and feared for his own soul. Perhaps he began to understand that Jesus would soon face the orange fires of hell in order to wrestle the keys away from the devil who'd held them entirely too long. Jesus Himself would suffer loss that we might be set free.

Co-Leader _____
Mark 14:53-65 **Slide 10 (Jesus blindfolded being beaten)**

55 The chief priests and the whole Sanhedrin were looking for evidence against Jesus so that they could put him to death, but they did not find any. 56 Many testified falsely against him, but their statements did not agree.

57 Then some stood up and gave this false testimony against him: 58 "We heard him say, 'I will destroy this man-made temple and in three days will build another, not made by man.'" 59 Yet even then their testimony did not agree.

60 Then the high priest stood up before them and asked Jesus, "Are you not going to answer? What is this testimony that these men are bringing against you?" 61 But Jesus remained silent and gave no answer.

Again the high priest asked him, "Are you the Christ, the Son of the Blessed One?"

62 "I am," said Jesus. "And you will see the Son of Man sitting at the right hand of the Mighty One and coming on the clouds of heaven."

63 The high priest tore his clothes. "Why do we need any more witnesses?" he asked. 64 "You have heard the blasphemy. What do you think?"

They all condemned him as worthy of death. 65 Then some began to spit at him; they blindfolded him, struck him with their fists, and said, "Prophesy!" And the guards took him and beat him.

Leader

Have you ever been spit on? It is one of the most insulting things anyone can do. The Creator that fashioned the glands to produce saliva was now being spit upon by the very creatures He had made and given life to. **Slide 11. (Pink)** Their clear spit combined with his blood to produce a pinkish color. Through the clear spit and His fresh wounds, we can see the bitterness and anger and rage in their own souls. And in ours. Forgive us for using what You have created in us to hurt You or another one that You have created.

Co-Leader _____
Matt 27:1-5   **Slide 12 (Sliver coins)**
27 Early in the morning, all the chief priests and the elders of the people came to the decision to put Jesus to death. 2 They bound him, led him away and handed him over to Pilate, the governor.
3 When Judas, who had betrayed him, saw that Jesus was condemned, he was seized with remorse and returned the thirty silver coins to the chief priests and the elders. 4 "I have sinned," he said, "for I have betrayed innocent blood."
"What is that to us?" they replied. "That's your responsibility."
5 So Judas threw the money into the temple and left. Then he went away and hanged himself.

Leader:

Into all this, we also see silver. **Slide 13. (Aluminum Foil)** Silver was the color of the coins that motivated Judas to betray his best friend. Silver was the color that lubed the wheels of the crucifixion. "The love of money is a root of all kinds of evil," the Bible warns. Let us be wary of silver's allure.

Co-Leader _____

Matt 27:11-18 **Slide 14 (Pilate and Jesus)**

11 Meanwhile Jesus stood before the governor, and the governor asked him, "Are you the king of the Jews?"

"Yes, it is as you say," Jesus replied.

12 When he was accused by the chief priests and the elders, he gave no answer. 13 Then Pilate asked him, "Don't you hear the testimony they are bringing against you?" 14 But Jesus made no reply, not even to a single charge — to the great amazement of the governor.

15 Now it was the governor's custom at the Feast to release a prisoner chosen by the crowd. 16 At that time they had a notorious prisoner, called Barabbas. 17 So when the crowd had gathered, Pilate asked them, "Which one do you want me to release to you: Barabbas, or Jesus who is called Christ?" 18 For he knew it was out of envy that they had handed Jesus over to him.

Leader:

    Slide 15. (Green) Envy. We don't think of it as that big of a deal. Certainly it's not a serious sin like some of the other biggies. And yet, it was envy that motivated the Jewish leaders to kill Jesus. He was getting attention and respect that they wanted for themselves. We often talk about someone being green with envy. Although the color is great for grass and trees, it looks horrible on our souls. Let's ask the Lord to reveal any envy within our own hearts that might cause us to hurt Him or someone else.

Co-Leader _____

Mark 15:11-20 **Slide 16 (Pilate and Jesus)**

11 But the chief priests stirred up the crowd to have Pilate release Barabbas instead.

12 "What shall I do, then, with the one you call the king of the Jews?" Pilate asked them.

13 "Crucify him!" they shouted.

14 "Why? What crime has he committed?" asked Pilate.

But they shouted all the louder, "Crucify him!"

15 Wanting to satisfy the crowd, Pilate released Barabbas to them. He had Jesus flogged, and handed him over to be crucified.

16 The soldiers led Jesus away into the palace (that is, the Praetorium) and called together the whole company of soldiers. 17 They put a purple robe on him, then twisted together a crown of thorns and set it on him. 18 And they began to call out to him, "Hail, king of the Jews!" 19 Again and again they struck him on the head with a staff and spit on him. Falling on their knees, they paid homage to him. 20 And when they had

mocked him, they took off the purple robe and put his own clothes on him. Then they led him out to crucify him.

Leader:

Slide 17. (Purple) See what green envy will do? And now, the normally royal color of purple is being used to mock the Highest King of all time. Purple was God's color for grapes and redbud blossoms and crocuses and irises. It is man's color for royalty. If they had just crucified Him it would have been bad enough, but the mockery and the abuse added to the suffering of our Savior more than we can imagine. **Slide 18 (Jesus in Purple robe)** The thorns that man's sin caused to grow on the earth were braided into a crown and placed on His holy sinless Head. Indeed, Isaiah was exactly right when he prophesied 800 years earlier that the Messiah would bear our sins.

Co-Leader _____
John 19:16-27 **Slide 19 (Jesus on Cross)**

So the soldiers took charge of Jesus. 17 Carrying his own cross, he went out to the place of the Skull (which in Aramaic is called Golgotha). 18 Here they crucified him, and with him two others — one on each side and Jesus in the middle. 19 Pilate had a notice prepared and fastened to the cross. It read: JESUS OF NAZARETH, THE KING OF THE JEWS. 20 Many of the Jews read this sign, for the place where Jesus was crucified was near the city, and the sign was written in Aramaic, Latin and Greek.

Leader:

Slide 20. (Brown) Brown was the color of the cross of Jesus. Taken from a descendent of a tree that Jesus Himself fashioned on day 3 of creation, it was cut down and formed into an instrument of brutality and torture. Never has brown wood been made into anything more hideous and awful than the day it was used to torture and kill its Creator. **Slide 21 (Jesus on Cross smaller with Brown outline)**

Let's Sing The Old Rugged Cross, number _____

Co-Leader _____ **Slide 22 (Slide of disciples grieving)**

25 Near the cross of Jesus stood his mother, his mother's sister, Mary the wife of Clopas, and Mary Magdalene. 26 When Jesus saw his mother there, and the disciple whom he loved standing nearby, he said to his mother, "Dear woman, here is your son," 27 and to the disciple, "Here is your mother." From that time on, this disciple took her into his home.

Leader

We don't know how many of Jesus' followers were actually on Skull Hill the day that Jesus died. Did all of the 11 eventually make their way there and watch from a distance? How many of the people who hailed Him as their King on Sunday were watching Him die there cruelly on Friday? John tells us that he himself was there along with Jesus' mother, Mary, and three other women. All of these had become followers and believers. All of them were bound to Him not by oaths and promises, but by strong cords of love and devotion. **Slide 23 Blue.** And now their hearts turned blue as they watched their son and friend die in humiliation. As the clear tears of heartbreak flowed down their faces, they were gripped with the grief and sadness not just of death, but of disappointment, disbelief, shock, and horror. Indeed, their hearts were as blue as any heart could ever be hurting for the one they loved.

Co-Leader _____ Luke 23:44-45

44 It was now about the sixth hour, and darkness came over the whole land until the ninth hour, 45 for the sun stopped shining.

Leader

Slide 24. (Cloudy Skies) For three hours that afternoon, the sun stopped shining. It was as if the Father could not bear to watch His Only Begotten Son suffer so painfully, so He turned out the lights. **Slide 25 (Grey).** Grey was the color of the sky that day as darkness descended over the entire landscape. Grey was the color that crept over the earth as we snuffed out the Light of the world. **Slide 26 (Hanging on the cross)**

Co-Leader _____ John 19:28-30

28 Later, knowing that all was now completed, and so that the Scripture would be fulfilled, Jesus said, "I am thirsty." 29 A jar of wine vinegar was there, so they soaked a sponge in it, put the sponge on a stalk of the hyssop plant, and lifted it to Jesus' lips. 30 When he had received the drink, Jesus said, "It is finished." With that, he bowed his head and gave up his spirit.

(Play a CD of the song "I walked today where Jesus walked.")

Leader:

And so ended the best life that ever lived. So ended the most beautiful of lives that ever lived. So ended the Creator of color. So ended the Creator of the Rainbow, God's Covenant of Promise. And while this may have been the end of one rainbow, it was the fulfillment of many promises. For there are two other colors we need to mention this evening. The most important colors of all.

Co-Leader _____: John 19:31-37
31 Now it was the day of Preparation, and the next day was to be a special Sabbath. Because the Jews did not want the bodies left on the crosses during the Sabbath, they asked Pilate to have the legs broken and the bodies taken down. 32 The soldiers therefore came and broke the legs of the first man who had been crucified with Jesus, and then those of the other. 33 But when they came to Jesus and found that he was already dead, they did not break his legs. 34 Instead, one of the soldiers pierced Jesus' side with a spear, bringing a sudden flow of blood and water. 35 The man who saw it has given testimony, and his testimony is true. He knows that he tells the truth, and he testifies so that you also may believe. 36 These things happened so that the scripture would be fulfilled: "Not one of his bones will be broken," 37 and, as another scripture says, "They will look on the one they have pierced."

Leader

Slide 27 (Jesus' hands being nailed with red outline). The best color of all is red. Red was the color of blood that He shed. When the thorns pierced His brow, it was red blood that flowed out. When He was ruthlessly flogged, the stains on the pavement were crimson. When the nails pierced His hands and feet, it was the bright red blood of life that exuded from His holy veins. And when the soldier pierced His side, red blood flowed forth.

Slide 28 (Red) From the time of the first sin in Eden's Garden, red blood was required to atone for sin. To pay the price for our disobedience and rebellion against God. In the Old Testament law, Moses described the red blood of sacrifice upon sacrifice that was needed to cover our sins. The entry to the holy temple and the tabernacle both were always stained red with blood.

Red blood was sprinkled on the Ark of the Covenant and also on the people of the covenant. Red has always been the color of the currency of forgiveness, of pardon. And red was the dominant color of Jesus' crucifixion. Without the shedding of blood there is no forgiveness of sin. But because Jesus shed His red blood, forgiveness is available to all who will receive it. I pray that you've received it tonight. **Slide 29 (Jesus hanging on cross with red outline).** If not, do so now as we sing the first 2 verses of number _____ When I Survey The Wondrous Cross.

Slide 30. (Black) We started with darkness tonight. Black is the absence of all color. It is empty. Black is the color of selfishness. When we see a black piece of paper, it's because the paper is absorbing all the colors that are shining on it and not letting any of them be reflected or shared back to us.

Slide 31. White. White on the other hand is the blending of all colors. A white paper is the most selfless in that it reflects all the colors back so we may see them. **Slide 32. (Photo of a prism with a white outline)** And as we combine all the colors of the crucifixion, the black night, the yellow disciples, the orange fire, the pink spit, the silver coins, the Green envy, the purple robe, the brown cross, the blue hearts, the grey sky, and the red blood, we end up with white. We are clean and pure because of what happened on Calvary that day. Our sins are washed away and we can now be pure and spotless before the white Lamb that was slain. **Slide 33. (Photo of lilies with white outline)** White is the color of Easter and indeed it reflects back to us all the beauty of the Risen Christ. But we'll wait till Sunday morning to celebrate all that. In the meantime, Let us reflect on the colors of the crucifixion that we might see God's mercy in each one. **Slide 34 (Jesus being laid in the tomb).**

Colors of the Cross
George Bowers

Brown was the color of the cross that He bore,
And purple the shade of the robe that He wore.
Yellow was Pilate, a coward was he,
Black was that day when Barabbas went free.
Blue were the hearts of the women who cared,
Orange were their eyes as they wept, as they stared.
Green were the envious leaders of men,
Who handed Christ over to pay for our sin.
Grey was the tint of the sky over head,
While His blood flowed out freely, a brilliant bright red.
Clear was the water that came from His side,
When the soldier had pierced Him to prove that He'd died.
But white is the color that He washed my dark soul,
He cleansed me completely, transformed me, made whole.
So gaze on this portrait as Jesus there dies,
Allow all these colors to come to your eyes.
Receive Christ today as you notice each hue,
For these colors are those of His great love for you!

Co-Leader _____ John 19:38-42

38 Later, Joseph of Arimathea asked Pilate for the body of Jesus. Now Joseph was a disciple of Jesus, but secretly because he feared the Jews. With Pilate's permission, he

came and took the body away. 39 He was accompanied by Nicodemus, the man who earlier had visited Jesus at night. Nicodemus brought a mixture of myrrh and aloes, about seventy-five pounds. 40 Taking Jesus' body, the two of them wrapped it, with the spices, in strips of linen. This was in accordance with Jewish burial customs. 41 At the place where Jesus was crucified, there was a garden, and in the garden a new tomb, in which no one had ever been laid. 42 Because it was the Jewish day of Preparation and since the tomb was nearby, they laid Jesus there.

Leader:

And so, with His promise of the Resurrection, we will leave Jesus in the tomb till we return on Sunday morning. **Slide 35 (Stone in front of door)**

Let's close by singing the last two verses of ____ tonight. When I Survey the Wondrous Cross.

Closing prayer.

Suggestion for Easter Sunday: Highlight white with white linen, white light, angels in white, etc.

Sponges

(Originally celebrated at Antioch Church of the Brethren on Good Friday 2016)

This Good Friday service provides insight into how one of
Jesus' closest disciples, Peter, reacted and responded throughout
Jesus' arrest, trial, and crucifixion. It also offers an understanding
of how Jesus sponged away our sin and hurt. If possible,
provide a small sponge for each participant.

Leader (slide)

Tonight we gather not to study or learn, not to serve or eat, not even to worship or praise, as much as to simply watch, feel, remember and mourn. Tonight we recognize the death of the Son of God whom we killed and who died for us. I invite you to clear your heart and mind this evening that we may enter into this experience totally unencumbered without the cares of the day. Take a few moments of silence right now to clear your hearts and minds.

At this time, we will sing _____ Near The Cross. Let us remain seated and sing together

(Silde-Cross)

Our desire is to stay Near the Cross tonight and to remember what our Lord experienced. Tonight, our story will be taken mostly from the book of Mark. In fact, many scholars believe Mark's Gospel should be called Peter's Gospel for it is believed that Mark simply wrote what Peter dictated to him about his life with Jesus. As such, _____ will read portions of Scripture and I will respond, perhaps as Peter might have, throughout that long night and day. We will pick up the story in Mark 14:26 immediately after the Last Supper in the Upper Room.

Co-Leader

26 When they had sung a hymn, they went out to the Mount of Olives.
27 "You will all fall away," Jesus told them, "for it is written:
"'I will strike the shepherd, and the sheep will be scattered.'
28 But after I have risen, I will go ahead of you into Galilee."

Leader (Slide of Jesus as Shepherd of the Sheep)

I didn't have a clue that night how severely our Shepherd would be struck. Indeed, He would be taken away even as the prophets declared, and when this would happen, all of us, His sheep, would indeed scatter. Instead of picking off individual lambs here and there, on this night and over the course of the next day, Satan made an all-out assault on our Shepherd Himself. I'm very embarrassed to say it, but when it did happen later that night, all of us sheep would run for own lives. I'm guessing you would have too.

Interestingly enough, within Jesus' prophecy of His impending death and our desertion is embedded an incredible promise of resurrection which we immediately dismissed until after He had done so. For He also promised to go ahead of us into

Galilee where He would regather His flock. Jesus was always going ahead of us and even tonight He continues to go ahead of you as well.

Co-Leader
29 Peter declared, "Even if all fall away, I will not."
30 "I tell you the truth," Jesus answered, "today — yes, tonight — before the rooster crows twice you yourself will disown me three times."
31 But Peter insisted emphatically, "Even if I have to die with you, I will never disown you." And all the others said the same.

Leader
I was determined to be true. I was determined to remain faithful to my Good Shepherd through thick and thin. I know not what course others may take, but as for me, I'll stand by You till the end.

"No," Jesus told me, "I'm afraid you won't. In fact, not only will you scatter with the rest of my sheep, you'll even deny that you know your Shepherd. Not once, not even twice, but three times. And all before the rooster crows at dawn tomorrow morning."

"Not me," I said. "Even if I have to die with You, I would never ever do that. You can count on me." And all the rest of our gang said, "Amen. We agree. We'll not desert You. You can count on us. We're true and faithful sheep. We'll be with You right on through it all."

Jesus knew we wouldn't do what we had boldly promised. In fact, He knew we **couldn't** do what we promised. He knew we would all fall away. And even though He knew it in His head, it didn't make His heart hurt any less. He had the same human emotions that we do and He felt the same pain of desertion and denial just like we would. Even of betrayal by one whose feet He had just washed earlier that evening and to whom He'd given a choice morsel.

Co-Leader
32 They went to a place called Gethsemane, and Jesus said to his disciples, "Sit here while I pray."

Leader (Slide of Jesus praying in Gethsemane)
Sounds like a reasonable request, doesn't it? Just sit and be with Me while I pray. I just need you close. I need your comfort and your presence. And **you** need to hear Me pray. How hard is it just to sit and pray?

Well, that depends on how much you've had to eat. When you last slept. What all you have to do. There are times when Jesus wants you to just sit with Him. Not to scurry about, not to sing, not to even read. But just to sit. That was one of those times. And tonight is one of those times.

Co-Leader
33 He took Peter, James and John along with him, and he began to be deeply distressed and troubled. 34 "My soul is overwhelmed with sorrow to the point of death," he said to them. "Stay here and keep watch."

Leader
Three of us sheep were especially close to our Shepherd and He wanted us to be especially close to Him as He faced His darkest hour. Whereas Jesus had been disturbed by the robbery in His Father's House of Prayer, He was not deeply distressed and troubled by it. Though we watched as He wept by Lazarus' tomb, He was not overwhelmed with sorrow to the point of death. Though He struggled when His cousin John was slaughtered by King Herod, He never agonized like He did in Gethsemane's olive press that night. He simply asked us to stay and keep watch with Him. Easy enough for any child, much less adult.

Co-Leader
35 Going a little farther, he fell to the ground and prayed that if possible the hour might pass from him. 36 "Abba, Father," he said, "everything is possible for you. Take this cup from me.

Leader
A few times in the Gospels, you are privileged to listen in on Jesus' prayer life. This is One of the most intimate and personal, however. He prayed for the hour to pass from Him. For the Cup of suffering to be taken away from Him. For this time of greatest pressure to be alleviated from Him.

He knew what He was facing. We didn't. He knew how much agony was in the cup that now was being handed to Him. He knew the bitter taste it contained and how sick it would make Him to drink it. Appealing to His Father of All Possibilities, He asked for a reprieve, for a way out. For another option if at all possible.

Jesus didn't like pain any more than you do. He didn't relish the thought of being beaten and tortured, abused and smacked, spit upon and laughed at. His nerves carried pain the same as ours do. His heart ached in identical fashion. Although He was the Son of God, He didn't get a "no pain" miracle to endure what was about to come His way.

What hurt most was the thought of becoming sin for us, and how, when He would do so, He would be shut out of the Father's intimate close loving presence for the first and only time in their eternal existence. Instead of feeling the Father's Love, He would experience the Father's wrath against all the evil He would be carrying. Instead of enjoying the Father's closeness, He would experience His alienation and separation. Instead of the splendors of heaven, He would descend to the lowest hell. Realizing all that was coming His way, He pled for another option. Any other way.

Co-Leader
"Yet not what I will, but what you will."

Leader
In true submission and humility He added, "Yet not what I will, but what You will." It's hard to comprehend such willing obedience in the face of such ultimate suffering. Such submission in the face of such grief. Such courage in the face of the universe's biggest battle. Yet not what I will, but what You will. Just like He taught us to pray in the Sermon on the Mount, Jesus now practiced what He preached by praying, "Thy will be done on earth even as it is in heaven."

Co-Leader
37 Then he returned to his disciples and found them sleeping. "Simon," he said to Peter, "are you asleep? Could you not keep watch for one hour? 38 Watch and pray so that you will not fall into temptation. The spirit is willing, but the body is weak."

Leader (Slide of Jesus praying while disciples are sleeping)
How disappointing it must have been for Jesus to find me, His staunchest supporter sleeping at His hour of greatest need. How sad it must have been for Him to find me to be a rod that would not support His weight when He tried to lean upon me. A potential comfort that provided none. Just one hour? Really? Watch and pray!

Those words echo down to you tonight. Watch and pray! That you might not fall into temptation. Whenever you fail to watch and whenever you fail to pray, you are the most susceptible to temptation. Believe me, I know!

You are too much like us disciples. Your spirits are more than willing! "Yes," you say, "We will follow Jesus anywhere! Any way! Any how!" But your flesh is just as weak as ours. You are ensnared by your physical limitations of rest, of food, of shelter, and so forth. Just like we were. Watch and pray always.

Co-Leader
39 Once more he went away and prayed the same thing. 40 When he came back, he again found them sleeping, because their eyes were heavy. They did not know what to say to him.

Leader
Everyone is allowed one free pass right? The first time it was unintentional. We simply messed up. "We promise we won't let it happen again. No sir. We're with you now." But the second time? Really? It was like He said, "I know you're sleepy, but hey, I've gotten less sleep than you have. Yes, I am God in the flesh, but I willingly submitted Myself to human limitations of sleep and hunger and thirst and such when I came to Bethlehem and entered a human body 33 years ago. My body works the same as yours does. And right now, I really need yours to stay awake and your souls to join me in prayer."

How often we boldly proclaim our willingness to labor for Jesus. To sacrifice for Him, to witness for Him, to do whatever for Him. But when the night begins to wear on, we become weary and go to sleep without fulfilling even His simplest request. "Could you not keep watch with Me one hour? Just one?"

Co-Leader
41 Returning the third time, he said to them, "Are you still sleeping and resting? Enough! The hour has come. Look, the Son of Man is betrayed into the hands of sinners. 42 Rise! Let us go! Here comes my betrayer!"

Leader
Oh wow. I can't believe I did it again. I can't believe my own failure. Oh Jesus, please forgive. I just couldn't help it. You understand don't you?

How our failure to even keep watch must have hurt Him. And how yours must today. Oh Jesus forgive us for failing to watch and pray with You. Empower us to do the supernatural and to enjoy sweet precious times of prayer with You in the late hours of night's darkness. **(Slide of soldiers coming with torches)**

"But now," He says, "it's too late! Get up! Not only did I have to carry the prayer burden, I also had to keep one eye turned to the distance for the authorities. And even now, they come to arrest me. See the light of their torches? Hear the stir of their voices? This is the hour of My betrayal."

Co-Leader
43 Just as he was speaking, Judas, one of the Twelve, appeared. With him was a crowd armed with swords and clubs, sent from the chief priests, the teachers of the law, and the elders.

Leader (Slide of Judas kissing Jesus)
What's that? Is that Judas with those guards? They must be friends then. He's on our side. And look, even now he's kissing Jesus. All is well. These men must be here to protect us. That's why they have all those swords and clubs.

Co-Leader
44 Now the betrayer had arranged a signal with them: "The one I kiss is the man; arrest him and lead him away under guard." 45 Going at once to Jesus, Judas said, "Rabbi!" and kissed him. 46 The men seized Jesus and arrested him.

Leader
Wait! What's going on here? They're not on our side! They're actually arresting Jesus! How dare they! And with a kiss from Judas. How could He? Jesus just washed His feet not more than an hour or two ago. Judas just embraced Jesus in the upper room. I never saw this coming.

Surely Jesus will perform some last minute miracle to achieve His escape. I can't wait to see what He does. In the meantime, we must defend Him as we promised. I might have fallen asleep, but I'm awake now and I'm going to do all in my power to protect Him, even if I have to die with Him. Just as I promised.

Co-Leader
47 Then one of those standing near drew his sword and struck the servant of the high priest, cutting off his ear.

Leader (Slide of Peter healing Malchus' ear)
Told ya! I got his ear! With the next swipe I'll get his throat! But before I could, Jesus stopped me and told me to put my sword away. He touched this man's bleeding ear and restored it right on the spot. You're not helping your cause here, Jesus! This man is arresting you and you're healing him? Surely you know this isn't a very effective battle plan.

Co-Leader
48 "Am I leading a rebellion," said Jesus, "that you have come out with swords and clubs to capture me? 49 Every day I was with you, teaching in the temple courts, and you did not arrest me. But the Scriptures must be fulfilled." 50 Then everyone deserted him and fled.

Leader
    If He's going to undo my defense, then I'm going to run. Next thing you know He'll be forgiving these guys. I love Him, but sometimes He just doesn't make sense. And even now He keeps referring to the Scriptures. I didn't have time to hang around and listen to which ones He meant. I only had time to run away. Just like He said I'd do.

Co-Leader
51 A young man, wearing nothing but a linen garment, was following Jesus. When they seized him, 52 he fled naked, leaving his garment behind.

Leader
    There's an odd snippet you don't hear much about. A streaker in Gethsemane. Who was this naked youngster? Rumor has it that it was the young man that would later become my scribe and write down this Gospel Story. A young man by the name of Mark. How else would anyone remember and record such a crazy detail?

Co-Leader
53 They took Jesus to the high priest, and all the chief priests, elders and teachers of the law came together. 54 Peter followed him at a distance, right into the courtyard of the high priest. There he sat with the guards and warmed himself at the fire.

Leader (Slide of Jesus warming himself by the fire)
    I tried to follow along after the posse…at a distance of course so as not to be arrested. It wouldn't be much help if I got arrested too. So I stayed in the shadows mostly with my hood over my head. I followed right into the high priest's courtyard and sat down with some of those who had just been in the garden. It was kind of cool that evening so I warmed myself by this common campfire.

Co-Leader
55 The chief priests and the whole Sanhedrin were looking for evidence against Jesus so that they could put him to death, but they did not find any. 56 Many testified falsely against him, but their statements did not agree.

Leader (Slide of Jesus being tried by Caiaphas)

You should have heard all the stories they told. I had to laugh at some of them. Ridiculous. Funny how none of them mentioned His many healings, or how He raised some from the dead. How He fed over 5,000 people beside the lake that day up in Galilee. Where were all these people? No one mentioned Bartimaeus to whom He had given sight or Jarius whose daughter He had raised from the dead. I wanted to speak up, but I just didn't feel the timing was right.

Co-Leader

57 Then some stood up and gave this false testimony against him: 58 "We heard him say, 'I will destroy this man-made temple and in three days will build another, not made by man.'" 59 Yet even then their testimony did not agree.

Leader

As often is the case, someone twisted Jesus's words. He never said that about the temple. He was actually talking about His body, in which truly dwelt the Presence of God. Not some building made of wood and stone. No wonder their testimony didn't agree. They weren't really listening. They heard only what they wanted to hear. Kind of like most people today.

Co-Leader

60 Then the high priest stood up before them and asked Jesus, "Are you not going to answer? What is this testimony that these men are bringing against you?" 61 But Jesus remained silent and gave no answer.

Leader (Slide of Jesus before Sanhedrin)

Why won't He speak? Why won't He defend Himself? You've got nothing to be ashamed of. Speak up, Jesus! You can turn these guys back on their heels! I've seen You go head to head with some of these very men before and leave them speechless, and even in front of a large crowd. Here in your own trial, can't You speak up? But He didn't.

Co-Leader

Again the high priest asked him, "Are you the Christ, the Son of the Blessed One?"
62 "I am," said Jesus. "And you will see the Son of Man sitting at the right hand of the Mighty One and coming on the clouds of heaven."

Leader

Oh wow. Now You speak. To the one charge that can seal Your fate. Why would You speak now? A simple I Am could be enough to convict You, but coming in the clouds of heaven? That's laying it on pretty thick isn't it? I know it's true and all us disciples know it's true, but saying something like that in front of this crowd could get You killed. Are You trying to get Yourself killed?

Where's your court appointed attorney? Where's your Advocate? Your legal defense team? Someone gave You some bad advice about how to testify in Your own defense. I was about to testify in His defense, but then…

Co-Leader

63 The high priest tore his clothes. "Why do we need any more witnesses?" he asked. 64 "You have heard the blasphemy. What do you think?"
They all condemned him as worthy of death.

Leader

Oh my. This is really getting desperate. Just a few hours ago, we were happily eating the Passover together and singing in the upper room. How did we go from there to here so quickly? From conversations about eternal kingdoms to earthly executions? And it seems to be unanimous. I waited too long to speak. Now I would have to act. Some way, some how.

Co-Leader

65 Then some began to spit at him; they blindfolded him, struck him with their fists, and said, "Prophesy!" And the guards took him and beat him.

Leader

I saw all of that from where I sat at the fire. I heard them hitting His face. I heard them mock and abuse Him. I watched as they drug Him away. It was time for me to move and take action.

Co-Leader

66 While Peter was below in the courtyard, one of the servant girls of the high priest came by. 67 When she saw Peter warming himself, she looked closely at him. "You also were with that Nazarene, Jesus," she said.

Leader (Slide of Peter being accused by the fire)

Before I could leave the fire, I nearly got busted. That servant girl. Where did she see me? She's going to blow my cover.

Co-Leader

68 But he denied it. "I don't know or understand what you're talking about," he said, and went out into the entryway.

Leader

Shew, that was close. If I'm going to get Him out of there, I can't get arrested myself. That would do no good.

Co-Leader

69 When the servant girl saw him there, she said again to those standing around, "This fellow is one of them." 70 Again he denied it.

Leader

Woman, would you please just shut up? What are you trying to prove? Just quit already. No, I don't know this Jesus.

Co-Leader

After a little while, those standing near said to Peter, "Surely you are one of them, for you are a Galilean."

Leader

Oh great. Now she's got the others convinced. I've got to convince them I'm not.

Co-Leader

71 He began to call down curses on himself, and he swore to them, "I don't know this man you're talking about."

Leader

That should do it. That should keep me free so I can somehow work out a plan to rescue Jesus.

Co-Leader

72 Immediately the rooster crowed the second time. Then Peter remembered the word Jesus had spoken to him: "Before the rooster crows twice you will disown me three times." And he broke down and wept.

Leader **(Slide of Peter crying with rooster in background)** (Crying)

Co-Leader
Announce Song: When I Survey The Wondrous Cross **verses 1-2** _____

Co-Leader
1 Very early in the morning, the chief priests, with the elders, the teachers of the law and the whole Sanhedrin, reached a decision. They bound Jesus, led him away and handed him over to Pilate.
2 "Are you the king of the Jews?" asked Pilate.
"Yes, it is as you say," Jesus replied.
3 The chief priests accused him of many things. 4 So again Pilate asked him, "Aren't you going to answer? See how many things they are accusing you of."
5 But Jesus still made no reply, and Pilate was amazed.

Leader (Slide of Jesus tied up before Pilate)
Just like His trial before the chief priests. He agrees with the one charge that will get Him killed and then He clams up about the others. Have you no legal mind?

Co-Leader
6 Now it was the custom at the Feast to release a prisoner whom the people requested. 7 A man called Barabbas was in prison with the insurrectionists who had committed murder in the uprising. 8 The crowd came up and asked Pilate to do for them what he usually did.
9 "Do you want me to release to you the king of the Jews?" asked Pilate, 10 knowing it was out of envy that the chief priests had handed Jesus over to him.

Leader (Slide of Pilate, Jesus, and Barabbas)
That should do it. Surely enough of the people He's helped will be here to demand His release. Even those who don't much know Him will certainly side **with** Him—since He's done nothing worthy of death. Many of these were out there Sunday waving palm branches and welcoming Him as their King. This is going to turn out alright after all.

Co-Leader
11 But the chief priests stirred up the crowd to have Pilate release Barabbas instead.

Leader

What? How can this be? No!! You can't make that choice! He's innocent! He's only helped people! Barabbas? Do you really want a murderer back out on the streets? Really? Think people!

Co-Leader

12 "What shall I do, then, with the one you call the king of the Jews?" Pilate asked them.

Leader

Let Him go also! Let Him go!! Please Just let Him go!!

Co-Leader

13 "Crucify him!" they shouted.
14 "Why? What crime has he committed?" asked Pilate.
But they shouted all the louder, "Crucify him!"

Leader (Slide of Jesus being rejected by the crowd)

How can they say this? What are they thinking? Just Sunday, the same crowd said they wanted Him to be their King! They shouted Hosanna and waved palm branches for Him. How can people be so fickle? Surely Pilate is a man of justice. Rome won't put an innocent man to death.

Co-Leader

15 Wanting to satisfy the crowd, Pilate released Barabbas to them. He had Jesus flogged, and handed him over to be crucified.

Leader

No!! It can't be!! Oh God, stop this!! Wake me up out of this bad dream. This nightmare. You've intervened many times in human history. Remember the Passover in Egypt? Remember David and Goliath? Remember Esther? Remember? Oh God, you've got to show up again! Come to save Jesus. He's your Son! He's Your representative!

Co-Leader

16 The soldiers led Jesus away into the palace (that is, the Praetorium) and called together the whole company of soldiers. 17 They put a purple robe on him, then twisted together a crown of thorns and set it on him. 18 And they began to call out to him,

"Hail, king of the Jews!" 19 Again and again they struck him on the head with a staff and spit on him. Falling on their knees, they paid homage to him.

Leader (Slide of Jesus being whipped)

This can't be happening to my Jesus. To my best friend and rabbi. To our leader and shepherd. Surely not, Oh God. Rome is better than this! I can't even recognize Him. His face is so smeared with blood. His back is so ripped to shreds. His whole body is so badly bruised. Is that really Jesus? He must be so miserable! Surely this is enough. No wonder He was praying so hard in the Garden last night. No wonder He asked us to watch and pray with Him. And we didn't. We failed Him. I failed Him. Oh God, please forgive me. Surely the guards will release Him after they get done torturing Him. That will be enough.

Co-Leader

20 And when they had mocked him, they took off the purple robe and put his own clothes on him. Then they led him out to crucify him. 21 A certain man from Cyrene, Simon, the father of Alexander and Rufus, was passing by on his way in from the country, and they forced him to carry the cross.

Leader (Slide of Jesus carrying the cross)

We'd walked these streets many times. But never with such heaviness of heart. We'd seen others crucified, but never someone we knew, much less our best friend. The Son of God. He keeps stumbling and falling under that heavy cross. He keeps tripping. Someone should help Him. Maybe this is my chance to slide in and let Him make a run for it. But no, they grabbed someone else. Another Simon. I'm useless.

Co-Leader

22 They brought Jesus to the place called Golgotha (which means The Place of the Skull). 23 Then they offered him wine mixed with myrrh, but he did not take it. 24 And they crucified him.

Leader (Slide of Jesus dying on the cross)

How many times we've passed this skull hill going into and out of Jerusalem. How many times we've commented on how evil it looks. Like staring the devil straight in the face. And now Jesus is being crucified on top of it. How can this be? He who helped fashion clothing to cover Adam and Eve's naked sin now hangs there naked and exposed Himself.

Nails driven deeply through the flesh of His holy hands and feet. All of mankind's unholiness. All of mankind's ugliness has been poured out upon the most Beautiful One. While He healed the guard's ear last night in the Garden, today His ears bleed profusely from the thorns in His crown. How could this happen? Crucifixion is for murderers and thieves, for liars and cheats, for whoremongers and prostitutes. Oh my. He's hanging there for me! For us! For you. For all of us!!

What You, my Lord, have suffered, Was all for sinners' gain;
Mine, mine was the transgression, But Yours the deadly pain.
Lo, here I fall, my Savior! 'Tis I deserve Your place;
Look on me with Your favor, grant me Your great grace.
(O Sacred Head Now Wounded)

Co-Leader
Dividing up his clothes, they cast lots to see what each would get. 25 It was the third hour when they crucified him. 26 The written notice of the charge against him read: THE KING OF THE JEWS.

Leader
Yes, He is my king! I gladly own His as my king! He is my Shepherd! He is my Sovereign! He is my God!! He's my Savoir! Even on the cross, He is my King!! Oh how pitiful to see Him hanging there like that. Oh how convicting. How humbling. How overwhelming.

Co-Leader
Let us sing verses 3-4 of When I Survey, number _____

Co-Leader
27 They crucified two robbers with him, one on his right and one on his left.

Leader (Slide of crowd at the foot of the cross)
Yes, they deserve it. In fact, Barabbas deserves to be there in the middle of them, not Jesus. This man should be flanked by angels. By cherubim and heavenly choirs. He's used to sitting at the right hand of God. Not despicable criminals.

Co-Leader
29 Those who passed by hurled insults at him, shaking their heads and saying, "So! You who are going to destroy the temple and build it in three days, 30 come down from the cross and save yourself!"

Leader

Inside, I'm secretly praying the same thing, but not in jest. Please, dear Jesus, please come down from this cross! Please come down and save yourself! Please come down so you can save us! Please come down and prove to all these idiots who You really are!! I know who You are, but something's gone very wrong. You can set this all back to right again if You want. I know You can. You are the Messiah. You are the Savior! But if You don't do it soon, You won't have a life left to save us with.

Co-Leader

31 In the same way the chief priests and the teachers of the law mocked him among themselves. "He saved others," they said, "but he can't save himself! 32 Let this Christ, this King of Israel, come down now from the cross, that we may see and believe." Those crucified with him also heaped insults on him.

Leader

These are the men who are supposed to show us the way of God. Who are supposed to model the Law of Moses. But they break it so openly. So obviously. So enjoyably.

Such verbal abuse. Isn't His humiliation enough? Must you rub this salt of sarcasm into His fresh wounds? Just shut up and let Him be. Let Him die without this abuse and these insults.

Co-Leader

33 At the sixth hour darkness came over the whole land until the ninth hour.

Leader   (Slide of Jesus on cross alone)

Something's happening. Maybe this is the turning point. Maybe He's caused this darkness so He can display His power. Surely He's going to come down at the last minute and whoop 'em all!

I had great trouble staying awake to pray last night, but now I have no trouble, even though it's dark. Ever since His arrest, I haven't stopped praying. Come on Jesus. Come on God.

Co-Leader

34 And at the ninth hour Jesus cried out in a loud voice, "Eloi, Eloi, lama sabachthani?"-which means, "My God, my God, why have you forsaken me?"

Leader

      What is that supposed to mean? Why would He say that? Surely He can't mean that. His Father would never forsake Him. Unless it's because of my sin that He carries. And yours. And that of all humans. Can it be? That for the first time in their eternal existence, He knows not the close intimate relationship with God His Father and God the Holy Spirit. For the first time ever, He knows what it feels like to be separated from His Father by sin. Now there is agony on His face.

Co-Leader

35 When some of those standing near heard this, they said, "Listen, he's calling Elijah." 36 One man ran, filled a sponge with wine vinegar, put it on a stick, and offered it to Jesus to drink. "Now leave him alone. Let's see if Elijah comes to take him down," he said.

Leader

      Don't be stupid. He's not calling Elijah. He's calling His Father. Elijah can't save Him and if God His Father doesn't do so soon, there won't be anything left to save.

Co-Leader

37 With a loud cry, Jesus breathed his last.

Leader

      No!! It can't be!! Come back! This can't be the end! He promised us eternal life! He promised power! He promised victory! This can't be the end of it all! It can't be!

Co-Leader

      At this time we'll sing the Old Rugged Cross from page _____ and as we do so, we need some ushers to pass the offering plates. Not so you can put something in, but so you can take something out. Please take one sponge from the plate as it is passed tonight as we sing.

Leader (Same Slide of Jesus on the cross alone)

      While Peter struggles with what he has just lived through, I'd like for us to focus on one detail Mark recorded that we often pay little mind to.

      We often think of what Jesus gave out during His crucifixion. Of His blood poured out for all mankind. Of His sweat and His agony that exuded from every pore of His body. Of His love and His grace that flowed even more freely than His blood. But have you ever thought of what He absorbed? In Mark's account of the crucifixion, He includes the sponge of wine vinegar that was offered to Him to drink.

We don't usually say much about this part of the story, but we should dwell on it particularly tonight. John tells us in his Gospel that the stick they put this sponge on was a stalk of the hyssop plant. The hyssop plant is **(photo of a hyssop plant)** a member of the mint family and has a strong odor. It commonly grew in rocky crevices in places other plants could not survive.

It was branches of the hyssop plant that Moses told the people to dip in the blood of the Passover lambs and then smear the top and sides of their doorframes with. Later, hyssop was used to dip in the blood of sacrificed birds and then to sprinkle on a person who had been healed of an infectious disease. Or on a home that had been cleansed of mildew.

And after David had sinned grievously and later confessed his sin and sought God's forgiveness, he pleaded in Psalm 51:7, Cleanse me with hyssop, and I will be clean; wash me, and I will be whiter than snow.

The role of hyssop was well established in cleansing from sin and impurity and it was no coincidence that hyssop was used to offer the sponge of wine vinegar to alieve Jesus' thirst.

The sponge, mentioned here, **(Slide-Photo of a sponge)** however, is unique to the story of Jesus' death. Nowhere else in the whole Bible do we find a sponge mentioned. Nowhere. But I think its presence here at Jesus' crucifixion is no coincidence.

We use sponges for a variety of reasons, but mostly to clean up. We wipe up counters and floors with sponges. We wash cars and houses with them. Some of us even use them to wash ourselves. In Jesus' day, they were used for washing too, but also to filter water, as early canteens, and even as padding inside the helmets of Roman Centurions.

Sponges are made of 66% empty space and work incredibly well at wicking up water. Various types of sponges are now used to absorb chemical spills and gasoline accidents. Types of sponges are included on every HAZMAT emergency vehicle because they are able to collect harmful substances and keep them out of streams, rivers, and wells. Sponges clean up our messes.

So while the sponge may have come out of a centurion's army helmet that afternoon and was then dipped in wine vinegar for the Savior, it symbolizes what the Savior did for that centurion, for Peter, and for all of us here tonight. For a few moments later, when He died on the cross, He absorbed our worst messes, our sin and filth. He sponged away our guilt and shame. He cleansed us of all unrighteousness and by His stripes, we are healed.

That day He absorbed all of our evil and violence. He took into Himself all of our pain and suffering. All of our bullying and abuse. Our fear, hostility, animosity, hatred, bitterness, greed, selfishness, pride. He took it all. Everything that mars and corrupts the human soul.

So tonight as you grip your sponge, imagine Christ sucking all of your sin out of you. Invite Him to do that for you. And thank Him for doing that when He died on the Cross.

Silent Prayer while piano plays softly.

Anyone want to offer a spoken prayer?

(Slide of person kneeling before the cross)
What language shall I borrow To thank You, dearest Friend?
For this Your dying sorrow, Your pity without end?
O make me Yours forever! And, should I fainting be,
Lord, Let me never, never, Outlive my love to Thee.
(Oh Sacred Head Now Wounded)

Let us sing together Beneath the Cross on Screen found on page _____

Co-Leader (Slide of Jesus' burial)
38 The curtain of the temple was torn in two from top to bottom. 39 And when the centurion, who stood there in front of Jesus, heard his cry and saw how he died, he said, "Surely this man was the Son of God!"
40 Some women were watching from a distance. Among them were Mary Magdalene, Mary the mother of James the younger and of Joses, and Salome. 41 In Galilee these women had followed him and cared for his needs. Many other women who had come up with him to Jerusalem were also there.
42 It was Preparation Day (that is, the day before the Sabbath). So as evening approached, 43 Joseph of Arimathea, a prominent member of the Council, who was

himself waiting for the kingdom of God, went boldly to Pilate and asked for Jesus' body. 44 Pilate was surprised to hear that he was already dead. Summoning the centurion, he asked him if Jesus had already died. 45 When he learned from the centurion that it was so, he gave the body to Joseph. 46 So Joseph bought some linen cloth, took down the body, wrapped it in the linen, and placed it in a tomb cut out of rock. Then he rolled a stone against the entrance of the tomb. 47 Mary Magdalene and Mary the mother of Joses saw where he was laid.

Leader

And we will leave Him there till we come back with the ladies on Sunday morning. Let us go out remembering His death for us.

Suggestion for Easter Sunday: Have Peter holding a piece of sponge that he picked up from beneath the cross as he shares his perspective on the resurrection.

Jesus' Cup

*This Service was originally celebrated on
Good Friday at Antioch Church of the Brethren 2019*

To prepare for this service, hand each participant a cup of some type.
It could be a coffee cup or even a paper or Styrofoam cup. Participants will take
an imaginary drink from this cup several times during the service.

As we gather this evening, I would remind you that our Good Friday service is a bit different than Sunday worship. Whereas Sunday services are generally upbeat and celebratory, this evening of the year is much more somber and a time for quiet reflection and pondering. To help us prepare for our time together, let's just pause for a few moments of silent prayer asking God to cleanse our minds and hearts of all the cares of the day and week and just a desire to focus on Jesus and His sacrifice tonight.

Silent Prayer

Dear Father:

We do pause here in the quietness of this hour in this sanctuary to reflect on the greatest act of love in human history. To reflect on the act that changed our eternal address and erased all our sin. To ponder the meaning and to feel the depth of Jesus' crucifixion. We ask you, Father, to give us the aid of your Holy Spirit. Help us to set aside our cares and our worries and experience Your presence tonight. In the Name of the Crucified One, Jesus Christ, we pray, Amen.

Let's turn to Hymn number _____ and sing the first and third verses of The Old Rugged Cross

Our journey to Golgotha tonight begins where Jesus' did the night before, in the upper room washing feet, sharing a meal and participating in the bread and the cup. Let me remind you of a few things Jesus said that night toward the end of their meal:

Matt 26:26-27:66
26 While they were eating, Jesus took bread, gave thanks and broke it, and gave it to his disciples, saying, "Take and eat; this is my body."
27 Then he took the cup, gave thanks and offered it to them, saying, "Drink from it, all of you. 28 This is my blood of the covenant, which is poured out for many for the forgiveness of sins. 29 I tell you, I will not drink of this fruit of the vine from now on until that day when I drink it anew with you in my Father's kingdom." 30 When they had sung a hymn, they went out to the Mount of Olives.

So after Jesus shares the cup of the New Covenant with them, He says He will not drink of it again until He drinks it anew in His Father's Kingdom. But He did have another cup to drink that night. In fact, I would say He had several cups yet to drink. **(Slide 1-A cup of some type.)**.The first came a short while later as Jesus prayed in Gethsemane at the base of the Mount of Olives. Matthew describes it this way:

Matt 26:31-35 Then Jesus told them, "This very night you will all fall away on account of me, for it is written:
"'I will strike the shepherd, and the sheep of the flock will be scattered.'
32 But after I have risen, I will go ahead of you into Galilee."
33 Peter replied, "Even if all fall away on account of you, I never will."
34 "I tell you the truth," Jesus answered, "this very night, before the rooster crows, you will disown me three times."
35 But Peter declared, "Even if I have to die with you, I will never disown you." And all the other disciples said the same.
36 Then Jesus went with his disciples to a place called Gethsemane, and he said to them, "Sit here while I go over there and pray." 37 He took Peter and the two sons of Zebedee along with him, and he began to be sorrowful and troubled. 38 Then he said to them, "My soul is overwhelmed with sorrow to the point of death. Stay here and keep watch with me."
39 Going a little farther, he fell with his face to the ground and prayed, "My Father, if it is possible, may this cup be taken from me. Yet not as I will, but as you will."
40 Then he returned to his disciples and found them sleeping. "Could you men not keep watch with me for one hour?" he asked Peter. 41 "Watch and pray so that you will not fall into temptation. The spirit is willing, but the body is weak."
42 He went away a second time and prayed, "My Father, if it is not possible for this cup to be taken away unless I drink it, may your will be done."
43 When he came back, he again found them sleeping, because their eyes were heavy.
44 So he left them and went away once more and prayed the third time, saying the same thing.
45 Then he returned to the disciples and said to them, "Are you still sleeping and resting? Look, the hour is near, and the Son of Man is betrayed into the hands of sinners. 46 Rise, let us go! Here comes my betrayer!"

The first cup Jesus had to drink that night was a cup full of disappointment. **(Slide 2-Jesus holding a cup.)** Say disappointment. After just promising to never fall away, they all did. They fell away in sleep and slumber. During His struggle in the Garden, when His soul was sorrowful even to the point of death, His closest friends were of no use whatsoever. They had crashed and were sleeping through Jesus' most difficult hour. When He needed them most, they gave Him the least. Even at His insistent request to watch with Him one hour, they could not, for their flesh was like ours. It was weak. And so they slept while Jesus wept and prayed and sweat great drops of blood.

Prayer: Jesus, we confess to You tonight that we have filled Your cup with disappointment too. Far too often, we have promised and failed to deliver. We have sworn and fallen asleep, vowed and reneged, pledged and defaulted. Forgive us. We are truly sorry. By Your Spirit's power, help us to never do so again.

Take a drink from Jesus' cup of disappointment tonight.

Let's sing the first and second verses of _____ When I Survey The Wondrous Cross

Picking up the story again, Matthew tells us
47 While he was still speaking, Judas, one of the Twelve, arrived. With him was a large crowd armed with swords and clubs, sent from the chief priests and the elders of the people. 48 Now the betrayer had arranged a signal with them: "The one I kiss is the man; arrest him." 49 Going at once to Jesus, Judas said, "Greetings, Rabbi!" and kissed him.
50 Jesus replied, "Friend, do what you came for."
Then the men stepped forward, seized Jesus and arrested him.

The second bitter cup Jesus had to drink that night was a cup of betrayal. **(Slide- A photo of another ancient cup.)** Say betrayal. More intentional and more damaging than disappointment and neglect, Judas' betrayal was deliberate as he premeditated the act that would turn Jesus over to His enemies. And received money for it no less. Having just washed his feet an hour or so before, having just offered him His broken body and shed blood, having shared ministry over the last three years, the cup of Judas' betrayal had to be a bitter one to drink. Even though Jesus knew who and how, actually swallowing the truth of it all must have been most distasteful. Especially having done so with a kiss, the most tender form of human affection. We humans somehow find a way to corrupt and contaminate all that we touch. Even so, Jesus absorbed the hurt and exchanged it for grace as we read about next.

51 With that, one of Jesus' companions reached for his sword, drew it out and struck the servant of the high priest, cutting off his ear.
52 "Put your sword back in its place," Jesus said to him, "for all who draw the sword will die by the sword. 53 Do you think I cannot call on my Father, and he will at once put at my disposal more than twelve legions of angels? 54 But how then would the Scriptures be fulfilled that say it must happen in this way?"
Luke adds that, "he touched the man's ear and healed him."

Blessing those who persecuted Him, Jesus returned love for hatred, grace for abuse, healing for injury. Drink the cup of betrayal tonight.

Unfortunately, there were other cups left to drink as well.
55 At that time Jesus said to the crowd, "Am I leading a rebellion, that you have come out with swords and clubs to capture me? Every day I sat in the temple courts teaching, and you did not arrest me. 56 But this has all taken place that the writings of the prophets might be fulfilled." Then all the disciples deserted him and fled.

The next cup was desertion. **(Slide-Another ancient cup)** Say desertion. Oh yes, He knew it would happen. He even told them it would. But that doesn't mean it hurt Him any less. To actually have your closest and best friends leave you high and dry, to turn tail and run had to be a difficult cup to drink. After spending three years together, sleeping under the stars together, healing, feeding, and teaching together. And having heard their assurances of loyalty just moments before, I'm sure Jesus had to swallow hard to gulp down the pain He felt as all of His disciples turned and fled.

Of course, that was a cup that would be refilled several times over that night. Peter, you remember, who promised "Even if I have to die with You, I will never disown You," denied three times that very night that he even knew Jesus. As if once was not enough and in addition to the cup of betrayal from Judas, Jesus had to repeatedly drink down 10 other cups of desertion, —one for each of the other disciples, and three more from Peter, the Rock.
Take a drink of Jesus' cup of desertion tonight.

Prayer: Oh God, forgive us for refilling the cup of desertion for You to drink. Forgive us for abandoning You and Your way when it becomes unpopular or inconvenient to do so. Forgive us we pray.

Let's sing the first and third verses of number ____ Beneath the Cross of Jesus

Matthew records this about what happened next:
57 Those who had arrested Jesus took him to Caiaphas, the high priest, where the teachers of the law and the elders had assembled. ..
59 The chief priests and the whole Sanhedrin were looking for false evidence against Jesus so that they could put him to death. 60 But they did not find any, though many false witnesses came forward.
Finally two came forward 61 and declared, "This fellow said, 'I am able to destroy the temple of God and rebuild it in three days.'"

62 Then the high priest stood up and said to Jesus, "Are you not going to answer? What is this testimony that these men are bringing against you?" 63 But Jesus remained silent. The high priest said to him, "I charge you under oath by the living God: Tell us if you are the Christ, the Son of God."

64 "Yes, it is as you say," Jesus replied. "But I say to all of you: In the future you will see the Son of Man sitting at the right hand of the Mighty One and coming on the clouds of heaven."

65 Then the high priest tore his clothes and said, "He has spoken blasphemy! Why do we need any more witnesses? Look, now you have heard the blasphemy. 66 What do you think?"

"He is worthy of death," they answered.

67 Then they spit in his face and struck him with their fists. Others slapped him 68 and said, "Prophesy to us, Christ. Who hit you?"

Another cup. This one of rejection. **(Slide of another cup.)** Say rejection. The very ones who should have recognized the Messiah didn't. The very ones who should have received Him, turned Him away. Take a swig of Jesus' cup of rejection.

And worse, they lied about Him. They served Him a cup of slander. **(Slide of another cup)** Say slander. Ever had anyone lie about you? Intentionally spread something false that ruined your reputation? Doesn't taste too good does it? It didn't to Jesus either. And He had a full cup of the worst flavor. And this was from people He loved. People who knew His Father's Word better than anyone. And they topped this cup off not with espresso cream, but the jalapenos of physical abuse. Spitting, hitting and slapping. Some of you know all too well what that tastes like too. How it burns going down. You yearn for relief. Drink of Jesus' slander and abuse.

And then mockery. **(Slide of another cup)** Say Mockery. Prophesy to us, who hit You? Being blindfolded, He couldn't see with physical eyes, but knowing all things, He knew perfectly well who served Him this cup. And He knew how the ingredients got into the cup they mixed and gave to Him. He knew that they had been physically abused and mocked somewhere along the way themselves. Perhaps by parents, maybe by superiors or bosses, or by neighbors or relatives. He absorbed their hatred, anger, persecution, physical aggression and mockery as He drank yet another cup filled with human suffering. Take a drink of the cup of mockery.

27 Early in the morning, all the chief priests and the elders of the people came to the decision to put Jesus to death. 2 They bound him, led him away and handed him over to Pilate, the governor. …

11 … Jesus stood before the governor, and the governor asked him, "Are you the king of the Jews?"

"Yes, it is as you say," Jesus replied.

12 When he was accused by the chief priests and the elders, he gave no answer. 13 Then Pilate asked him, "Don't you hear the testimony they are bringing against you?" 14 But Jesus made no reply, not even to a single charge — to the great amazement of the governor.

Usually, whenever one must drink something distasteful and bitter, the person complains, growls, or resists. Jesus did none of that. He took it all in and responded with confident silence. Instead of protesting, promising revenge, and calling His lawyer, He quietly drank and waited for the next cup. He didn't have to wait long.

15 Now it was the governor's custom at the Feast to release a prisoner chosen by the crowd. 16 At that time they had a notorious prisoner, called Barabbas. 17 So when the crowd had gathered, Pilate asked them, "Which one do you want me to release to you: Barabbas, or Jesus who is called Christ?" 18 For he knew it was out of envy that they had handed Jesus over to him.

19 While Pilate was sitting on the judge's seat, his wife sent him this message: "Don't have anything to do with that innocent man, for I have suffered a great deal today in a dream because of him."

20 But the chief priests and the elders persuaded the crowd to ask for Barabbas and to have Jesus executed.

21 "Which of the two do you want me to release to you?" asked the governor.

"Barabbas," they answered.

22 "What shall I do, then, with Jesus who is called Christ?" Pilate asked.

They all answered, "Crucify him!"

23 "Why? What crime has he committed?" asked Pilate.

But they shouted all the louder, "Crucify him!"

24 When Pilate saw that he was getting nowhere, but that instead an uproar was starting, he took water and washed his hands in front of the crowd. "I am innocent of this man's blood," he said. "It is your responsibility!"

25 All the people answered, "Let his blood be on us and on our children!"

26 Then he released Barabbas to them.

Behold the cup of injustice. **(Slide of another cup)** Say injustice. We humans are experts at mixing that one. So often we let the guilty go free while condemning the innocent. We've done it with slavery, we've done it with economics, we've done it because of payoffs and money, we've done it to gain favor with others, and we've done it for spite. Sometimes we've even done it for sport. We bottle this drink and sell it to the poor and the outcasts. Many have drunk from this cup down through the ages, but none more so than Jesus that day. For He of all people was most innocent. Completely innocent. Most deserving of acquittal and freedom. And Barabbas was most guilty. Most deserving of death and condemnation. And yet Barabbas was freed and Jesus sentenced. This cup too had to be difficult to sip, but Jesus upended it, drank it down to its dregs and then went on to the next. Drink the cup of injustice tonight.

Prayer: Dear God, where we have been unjustly treated, heal our wounded hearts. And help us to forgive those responsible. Forgive us for our injustice to You and to our fellow human beings thus adding yet more to Your cup. Amen.

Matthew says, "But he had Jesus flogged, and handed him over to be crucified."

Jesus' next cup was one He'd already had a sip of-physical abuse. **(Slide of another cup)** Say abuse. Only this time it was mixed triple and quadruple strength as they flogged Him mercilessly. Hit after hit after hit. This cup was more like an entire pitcher. Was there no glimmer of God's image in them anywhere? No speck of mercy and compassion? Apparently not as they kept filling cup after cup of torture at the whipping post. The Romans had become experts at mixing this drink and knew how to make it just strong enough to inflict the most pain without causing one to pass out from the dose. The whip made from the leather of a bull He Himself had fashioned. The bone fragments woven into it from a sheep He designed. Blood, the liquid of life that He engineered flowed freely and liberally from the whelps on His exposed back. Anger, an emotion He gave to mankind to respond to injustice and sin now turned into rage against their Creator. This cup had so many nasty tastes it was very difficult to finish. Drink from His cup of physical abuse.

Let's sing the third verse of When I Survey on page _____.

27 Then the governor's soldiers took Jesus into the Praetorium and gathered the whole company of soldiers around him. 28 They stripped him and put a scarlet robe on him, 29 and then twisted together a crown of thorns and set it on his head. They put a staff in his right hand and knelt in front of him and mocked him. "Hail, king of the Jews!" they said. 30 They spit on him, and took the staff and struck him on the head again and again. 31 After they had mocked him, they took off the robe and put his own clothes on him. Then they led him away to crucify him.

Here is the second round of mockery. **(Slide of same cup used for mockery earlier.)** Only this one had a double shot of sarcasm. Say sarcasm. Nakedness, scorn, disdain too for extra flavor. Some of you have had a taste of these. Prancing around proud of their clever crown, robe, and staff. Kneeling before Him in artificial honor. One day they will and it won't be pretend. He could have grasped the cup and poured it back on all their heads. In a split second He could have turned the tables and forced it down their own disrespectful throats, but instead He willingly gripped it, raised it to His lips and felt it burn as it went down into His soul. If only that were all. Drink from this cup of sarcasm and scorn.

33 They came to a place called Golgotha (which means The Place of the Skull). 34 There they offered Jesus wine to drink, mixed with gall; but after tasting it, he refused to drink it.

This was a bit of pain killer. Something to wash the bitterness from His mouth and mask the taste of what was coming next. But He would have none of it. No, He would drink the full strength of the cups set before Him. He would endure the full wrath, the full effects, the full dose of whatever was yet to come.

35 When they had crucified him, they divided up his clothes by casting lots. 36 And sitting down, they kept watch over him there. 37 Above his head they placed the written charge against him: THIS IS JESUS, THE KING OF THE JEWS. 38 Two robbers were crucified with him, one on his right and one on his left. 39 Those who passed by hurled insults at him, shaking their heads 40 and saying, "You who are going to destroy the temple and build it in three days, save yourself! Come down from the cross, if you are the Son of God!"
41 In the same way the chief priests, the teachers of the law and the elders mocked him. 42 "He saved others," they said, "but he can't save himself! He's the King of Israel! Let him come down now from the cross, and we will believe in him. 43 He trusts in God. Let God rescue him now if he wants him, for he said, 'I am the Son of God.'" 44 In the same way the robbers who were crucified with him also heaped insults on him.
45 From the sixth hour until the ninth hour darkness came over all the land. 46 About the ninth hour Jesus cried out in a loud voice, "Eloi, Eloi, lama sabachthani?"-which means, "My God, my God, why have you forsaken me?"

This was the cup He most dreaded. **(Slide of another cup)** He'd drunk the cups of suffering and pain, the cups of disappointment and betrayal. He'd downed the shots of mockery, rejection, torture, and injustice as though they were iced tea. But this one was most difficult to swallow.

What was in this cup? Your sin and mine. Say my sin. All our lies, gossip, hatred and bitterness. Our envy, lust, idolatry, and selfishness. All our complaining and worry and rage, all our dishonoring of the Sabbath day and of our parents. Our lack of love, failure to give. All of yours and all of mine. All of ours in this room. That cup's getting pretty full, isn't it? Now, pause to consider all the sins that humans have ever done because they were all in Jesus' cup that night. Estimates are that over 100 billion people have lived on the earth over time. If each one of us only sinned once, and each sin was equal to one drop of liquid Jesus had to drink, that would still equal well over 1 million gallons of water. That's over three times the amount of water in the Great Salt Lake and it is much nastier. That's if each of us just sinned once in our lives. And so imagine all the sins you've already done today. Already this week. Already this year. And you quickly have more water than exists in the entire world. And all of it tasting nastier than anything He'd already drunk. All of it more caustic than battery acid. All of it more sour than a lemon. For each drop draws the Father's wrath.

No wonder He prayed that this cup might pass from Him. Each drop contaminated by our sin. Each sin separating Him from the perfection of the Father. The only time ever when He couldn't be in the Father's direct presence. No wonder He prayed not to drink it. "Nevertheless, not my will but Thine be done."

50 And when Jesus had cried out again in a loud voice, he gave up his spirit.

No wonder He died. That cup would kill anyone and everyone. And indeed sin had killed everyone since time began. Everyone since Eden. And now He drank it that we might not have to.

Remember when we were kids and got sick and mom made us take some bitter medicine? Paregoric. Or something worse. We didn't want to drink it. We turned away. We sealed our lips. We wailed and carried on. Eventually we drank it and it made us better. Jesus didn't wail or pitch a fit, but He did ask the Father if there might be some other way. You see, He's not the one who needed the medicine. He wasn't the one who was sick. You were. I was. When He eventually did drink the bitter cup, **we** got better. By **His** stripes **we** were healed.

No one forced it down His throat. No one made Him drink it. He did it willingly that we might be forgiven, that we might be able to spend eternity in His presence. That we might not have to pay for our own sin. Don't drink this one for He drank all of yours for you.

Jesus drank your cup and mine that day on Calvary. He took into Himself all the sinful things that we ever did, thought, or said. Paul says, (2 Cor 5:21) "God made him who had no sin to be sin for us, so that in him we might become the righteousness of God." Let me finish Matthew's account of that day when God's Creatures crucified their Creator. Matt 27:57-66

57 As evening approached, there came a rich man from Arimathea, named Joseph, who had himself become a disciple of Jesus. 58 Going to Pilate, he asked for Jesus' body, and Pilate ordered that it be given to him. 59 Joseph took the body, wrapped it in a clean linen cloth, 60 and placed it in his own new tomb that he had cut out of the rock. He rolled a big stone in front of the entrance to the tomb and went away. 61 Mary Magdalene and the other Mary were sitting there opposite the tomb.

62 The next day, the one after Preparation Day, the chief priests and the Pharisees went to Pilate. 63 "Sir," they said, "we remember that while he was still alive that deceiver said, 'After three days I will rise again.' 64 So give the order for the tomb to be made secure until the third day. Otherwise, his disciples may come and steal the body and tell the people that he has been raised from the dead. This last deception will be worse than the first."

65 "Take a guard," Pilate answered. "Go, make the tomb as secure as you know how." 66 So they went and made the tomb secure by putting a seal on the stone and posting the guard.

Jesus prayed that the cup might pass from Him, but it did not. Indeed, His cup that night was refilled many times. Filled with disappointment, betrayal, desertion, mockery, slander, sarcasm, rejection, abuse, and injustice. All of it variations of our various forms of sin. In the end, the cup of our sin had the same effect on Him as it did and does on us. It killed Him. And as a result they buried Him in a rich man's tomb and the Jewish leaders even insisted that it be sealed with a heavy stone to prevent any collusion, corruption, or scandal. And so it was. We will leave Jesus there tonight and tomorrow and return on Sunday bright and early to find whatever we might. In the meantime, let's continue to reflect on God's love that gave us His Son, that willingly drank our cup and that willingly died our death that we might go free to live forevermore.

Alas and did my Savior bleed and did my Sovereign die? Would He devote His sacred Head for such a worm as I? Was it for crimes that I have done, He groaned up on the tree? Amazing pity, grace unknown and love beyond degree.

Take some time of silent prayer to thank Him for drinking the whole cup of your sins.

Prayer: Dear Gracious God. Loving Father, Dying Son, Thank You for drinking all those cups for us. Thank You for loving us enough to take our place. Thank You for suffering and enduring and dying that we might live. Help us to never take lightly the price You paid for our souls. We ask in Jesus Name, Amen.

Let's sing all four verses of When I Survey on page _____.

Suggestion for Easter Sunday: One could use a "Victor's Cup" trophy or perhaps a cup with champagne or something similar for the ultimate victory.

Beneath The Cross Of Jesus

This Service was originally celebrated at

Antioch Church of the Brethren on Good Friday, 2018

As we gather to remember our Lord's death this evening, I would invite you to check to be sure that your cell phones are silenced so that we may focus ourselves entirely on Jesus' last few hours tonight.

To help us center our minds on the purpose of our time together this evening, please remain seated and turn to page _____, and let's sing together the first and third verses of Near The Cross.

Prayer

As you know, this day is known as Good Friday. A good day for us humans, but a bad day for our Savior. We are forever grateful for Jesus' sacrifice on the cross, pouring out His red life's blood to pay for our sin, and tonight we want to take some time to dwell on that, to meditate upon it, to appreciate it, to sorrow for it, and to commemorate it that we might be able to properly celebrate His resurrection on Sunday.

Let's listen to John's description of the events of that first Good Friday.

Reader _____

John 19:15-42

15 But they shouted, "Take him away! Take him away! Crucify him!"
"Shall I crucify your king?" Pilate asked.
"We have no king but Caesar," the chief priests answered.
16 Finally Pilate handed him over to them to be crucified. So the soldiers took charge of Jesus. 17 Carrying his own cross, he went out to the place of the Skull (which in Aramaic is called Golgotha). 18 Here they crucified him, and with him two others — one on each side and Jesus in the middle.
19 Pilate had a notice prepared and fastened to the cross. It read: JESUS OF NAZARETH, THE KING OF THE JEWS. 20 Many of the Jews read this sign, for the place where Jesus was crucified was near the city, and the sign was written in Aramaic, Latin and Greek. 21 The chief priests of the Jews protested to Pilate, "Do not write 'The King of the Jews,' but that this man claimed to be king of the Jews."
22 Pilate answered, "What I have written, I have written."
23 When the soldiers crucified Jesus, they took his clothes, dividing them into four shares, one for each of them, with the undergarment remaining. This garment was seamless, woven in one piece from top to bottom.
24 "Let's not tear it," they said to one another. "Let's decide by lot who will get it."
This happened that the scripture might be fulfilled which said, "They divided my garments among them and cast lots for my clothing." So this is what the soldiers did.

25 Near the cross of Jesus stood his mother, his mother's sister, Mary the wife of Clopas, and Mary Magdalene. 26 When Jesus saw his mother there, and the disciple whom he loved standing nearby, he said to his mother, "Dear woman, here is your son," 27 and to the disciple, "Here is your mother." From that time on, this disciple took her into his home.

28 Later, knowing that all was now completed, and so that the Scripture would be fulfilled, Jesus said, "I am thirsty." 29 A jar of wine vinegar was there, so they soaked a sponge in it, put the sponge on a stalk of the hyssop plant, and lifted it to Jesus' lips. 30 When he had received the drink, Jesus said, "It is finished." With that, he bowed his head and gave up his spirit.

31 Now it was the day of Preparation, and the next day was to be a special Sabbath. Because the Jews did not want the bodies left on the crosses during the Sabbath, they asked Pilate to have the legs broken and the bodies taken down. 32 The soldiers therefore came and broke the legs of the first man who had been crucified with Jesus, and then those of the other. 33 But when they came to Jesus and found that he was already dead, they did not break his legs. 34 Instead, one of the soldiers pierced Jesus' side with a spear, bringing a sudden flow of blood and water. 35 The man who saw it has given testimony, and his testimony is true. He knows that he tells the truth, and he testifies so that you also may believe. 36 These things happened so that the scripture would be fulfilled: "Not one of his bones will be broken," 37 and, as another scripture says, "They will look on the one they have pierced."

38 Later, Joseph of Arimathea asked Pilate for the body of Jesus. Now Joseph was a disciple of Jesus, but secretly because he feared the Jews. With Pilate's permission, he came and took the body away. 39 He was accompanied by Nicodemus, the man who earlier had visited Jesus at night. Nicodemus brought a mixture of myrrh and aloes, about seventy-five pounds. 40 Taking Jesus' body, the two of them wrapped it, with the spices, in strips of linen. This was in accordance with Jewish burial customs. 41 At the place where Jesus was crucified, there was a garden, and in the garden a new tomb, in which no one had ever been laid. 42 Because it was the Jewish day of Preparation and since the tomb was nearby, they laid Jesus there.

Jesus was and is the Lamb of God who takes away our sin and just a moment ago we sang that again. In the song we also prayed for God to bring the scenes of the cross before us and for us to continuously live in the shadow of the cross. To help us do that tonight, we will be listening in on the thoughts of several individuals as they pause beneath the cross of Jesus. Our first individual is the Disciple Jesus loved, John, the Son of Zebedee.

John: _____

Oh my dear friend Jesus. My close and cherished friend. How can this be? He wasn't just my teacher, He was my best friend. Just last night I sat beside Him at supper. We dipped our bread in the same bowl. We ate from the same loaf and we drank from the same cup. Just last night we prayed in the Garden together. How could this have happened?

After His arrest last night in the Gethsemane, Peter and I tried to keep up with the crowd. We followed them to Caiaphas' house and I even got us inside. I know Caiaphas personally and I got us admitted. We watched in horror as witness after witness came forward to accuse Jesus of tons of things He never did. Thankfully, none of them stuck until one man said he had heard Jesus say He was going to destroy the temple. That got their attention. When another agreed, that's all it took and just like that they took Him away to Pilate. Somehow, I don't think Jesus was really talking about the big temple made of stone because He pointed to His body when He made that comment.

Anyway, when they took Him away, I got out of there. I could tell by the atmosphere of the crowd that this wasn't going well. I went to find the others to see if we could rally some support, but all had scattered in different directions like a flock of sheep without a shepherd.

By the time I caught up with Jesus again, He was being nailed to a cross. I caught a glimpse of His Mother on the other side and made my way to her to try to console her as she wailed and wept. Several of the soldiers and Jewish leaders gave me lots of dirty looks, but at that point I really didn't care.

Once they hung Him up, Jesus spoke some of His last words to me and His mom. "Woman, behold your son, Son behold your mother," he said. Even in death, He cared about others and kept the Commandments by honoring His mother. I guess I'll take her into my home now. It's really an honor to do so. It's the least I can do to honor Jesus who has done so much for me as I stand here beside her beneath the cross of Jesus.

Sing Verse 1 Beneath the Cross of Jesus

Not all who were there beneath Jesus' cross were upset by what they saw. Some were very happy, at least for a few days. Listen to what the High Priest Caiaphas has to say Beneath the Cross of Jesus:

Caiaphas _____

Serves Him right. He comes in here driving out our livestock, overturning our tables, turning the crowds against us. Let this be a lesson to all. No man dare cross us Jewish leaders or you'll get what you deserve.

The ironic thing is His name. It's Jesus. It means, the Lord saves. If His Lord really does save, let Him save Him now! In fact, Let Him come and take Him down off the cross. If He is such a healer, let Him heal those bleeding wounds in His own hands and feet.

He claimed to be a King. And to have a kingdom. A kingdom of thorns. That's what He has. That's all He'll ever have. And that's a fitting crown for His rebellious head.

This should squelch any resistance. It should send a message loud and clear to all who dare stand against us. On Sunday, He rode in here acting all high and mighty. Many of His followers hailed Him as a king, a Messiah, a deliverer.

Now He can't even deliver Himself. What a joke. What a fraud. Once hailed, now nailed! In three days time, He'll be completely forgotten. His disciples who started running in the garden last night will keep running if they know what's good for them. Without a leader, they're sure to disband and give up. One of them even helped us arrest Him! He's the lucky one to at least get 30 pieces of silver out of it.

Didn't He realize that with influence and power come responsibility? He should have used it wisely. Just a few days ago He went to our temple and created such a scene. Stirring up the sheep and cattle and sending them running all over the place and turning over the tables of our money changers. How dare He! This ought to make His puny followers think twice before they try anything else.

He even said He would destroy the temple and raise it up again in three days. Ha! He never got it destroyed, much less a stone to rebuild it. His foolish life is over and his foolish teaching is snuffed out. I'm so glad this is the end of Him. He's caused us enough trouble and kept me awake enough nights. I'm so relieved that all of this is finally over. Thank goodness.

Now that Jesus is almost dead, I feel safe and secure in my power and position here beneath His cross. What about you?

Caiaphas thoughts Beneath The Cross:
Beneath the cross of Jesus, I pause but to reflect
On ways that I have hurt my Lord, both passive and direct.
He died to save me from my sin, but I have hurt Him so,
Forgive me Jesus, for your love is greater than I know.

Indeed, depending on our perspective, we each respond differently to the cross of Jesus. Let's hear from Mary Magdalene.

Mary Magdalene _____

What is happening? What on earth is happening? How can this be? He healed me of my illness, drove seven demons out of me, delivered me from hopeless bondage and now they're killing Him?

I've done so many evil things, sinned so much in my past, but He forgave me of it all. Instead of judging me like everyone else, when I confessed, He forgave. Instead of looking down on me, He believed in me. He cared for me. He encouraged me. He blessed me. If He can forgive me, He can forgive anyone. Even you.

But where are His disciples? Where is justice? Where is God in all this? How could this happen? I may not know all there is to know about our Scriptures and our law, but I know this is wrong! I know it is! This man is like no other! He is different I tell you. He is the Messiah, I know it. God has revealed it to me. How could they thwart God's plan and kill Him like this? Oh dear God, do something! Do something! Please do something!!

Peter, do something! John, Do something! Somebody, do something! Passover is supposed to be a time of celebration, how could they kill any man, especially **this** man on Passover? Doesn't anyone care? Somebody please do something here beneath the cross of Jesus!

Beneath The Cross Verse three.

Can you indeed see the dying form of the One who suffered there on the cross for you? Do you see there the wonder of His glorious love and your own unworthiness? You're not the only one. Listen as Barabbas stops briefly to reflect:

Barabbas _____

Wow, there's a dose of reality. That really should be me up there on that cross. But in some unbelievable twist of fate, Pilate released me and killed Him. It all happened so fast, I still can't hardly believe it's all true, but the blood running from His hands and feet assures me that it is. Those should be **my** hands and **my** feet and **my** nails. That should be **my** blood. That should be **my** cross.

I think I heard His Name was Jesus? I don't know for sure, but even for a hardened murderer like me, it makes you stop and think. I woke up this morning in my prison cell fully expecting to be dead before sundown and now I'm free as a bird. Meanwhile, this man, whom apparently has done nothing deserving of death, is on His last hour. How does something like this happen? Why does something like this happen?

I wonder if He was born to take **my** place? I wonder if He was born to die for me? It almost seems like it. There's a part of me that feels really guilty. I hadn't really felt that before, but now that I stopped here beneath the cross of Jesus, I feel it very strongly.

I can go free. I can start over. I can go out and murder again if I like or I can go a different route and do good to others. My slate was wiped clean when this Man took my punishment. This is a rare and golden opportunity. What should I do? What would you do? What will you do?

I heard something in passing about this man being a well-known teacher. Perhaps I should check out His teachings to see what He had to say that got Him into so much trouble. Perhaps you should too. One thing I know, after standing here beneath this cross, I will never be the same.

Barabbas Thoughts Beneath The Cross
Upon the Cross of Jesus, I see my substitute
The One on whom my guilt was laid, my debt, God did impute
It should be me upon that tree, with nails through hands and feet,
I'll live for Jesus evermore and give Him each heartbeat.

Four different people, four very different perspectives. Let's listen now to another, that of Jesus' own mother, Mary:

Mary _____

I can't believe my Son, my firstborn, is hanging on a cross! Before He was ever born, the angel promised that He would be the Messiah, a special Son of God. I know very personally that He is different from every other human who ever lived for His conception was by the Holy Spirit, not by Joseph or by any other man. How then could God allow Him to die? He was supposed to support me in my old age. He was to deliver Israel and usher in the Kingdom of God. He spoke of it often. He was the brightest star in our family, but now this.

We tried to warn Him. Back up in Galilee, his brothers and I told Him to cool it and that His words and actions would get Him into trouble. And now they have. Eventually I changed my mind. Eventually I came around and began to listen and follow Him. I even encouraged others to do the same.

After what I saw He did at that wedding up in Cana a few years back. He instantly turned about 150 gallons of regular water into the finest wine any of us had ever tasted. But now all that wine is gone and all that's left is an empty wineskin hanging up there on the cross.

When Joseph and I dedicated Him at the temple when He was only 8 days old, this old prophet Simeon prophesied, that, "This child is destined to cause the falling and rising of many in Israel, and to be a sign that will be spoken against, so that the thoughts of many hearts will be revealed." That has all happened. He has been and is being spoken against right now and the cruel wicked hearts of our leaders are being clearly revealed.

But he also promised something else that day that sent a chill through my spine then. I didn't know what he meant, but now I do, for he promised, "A sword will pierce your own soul too." It has… and it is… and it hurts.

I want to smack those Jewish leaders standing over there making fun of Him. How can they do that? Have they no respect even in death? But that won't help Jesus. If only I could swab His brow. If only I could put some salve on the gaping wounds in His bleeding back. If only I could give Him a drink or a little food.

If only I could hold His dear head in my lap as I did when He was a child and sing Him softly to sleep. There, there, now, it will be alright. But it's not alright! It's all wrong! In just a few short moments my Son will be dead! I should've stopped Him. I should have. As a mom, I just want to make it all better. To make it not hurt anymore. But there's nothing I can do but weep…. and wish…. and pray, here beneath the cross of my son Jesus.

Beneath the Cross of Jesus Verse 2

What would you do for Jesus if you had been there? More importantly, what are you doing for Him now? What will you do for Him?

We don't know for sure if Malchus was actually at the cross, but there's good reason to believe he probably was. If so, his thoughts might have been something like this:

Malchus _____

I'm so mixed up I don't know what to think. I was so convinced that this was the right thing to do last night when I went along to arrest Jesus. Anyone who disgraced my master, the high priest Caiaphas, the way He had, deserved everything he got. I couldn't wait to get Him in chains and drag Him into court and let justice be done.

But then one of His men came at me out of the dark. I could tell he hadn't used a sword much or I'd be dead today. Instead, he just sliced off my ear. It bled and bled as I drew my sword to send that scrawny fisherman into eternity. But before I could, Jesus, the One we were arresting, touched my ear and suddenly it stopped bleeding. .. It stopped hurting. .. It stopped ringing… It started hearing again right away as if nothing had happened. I was stunned and I still am.

While the others went ahead and shackled Him, I kept trying to make sense of it all. How could this be? Nobody can do that. Not even the best doctors. Not even my master, the High Priest. One would have to be some sort of God to do that.

It was my responsibility to help guard Him throughout his trials until He was handed over to the Romans. And the whole time, I kept trying to make sense of it all.

Why would one I was arresting heal me? Whenever I've ever arrested anyone before, they always hated me. They glare and stare and I love it. But He was different. Whenever our eyes met, I could see love and compassion. How could He love even His enemy?

Even after I turned Him over to Pilate's men, I continued to follow to see what was going to happen. Even though we'd all been coached to shout "Crucify!" when Pilate asked us what to do with Him, I just couldn't shout along.

And now as I stand here beneath His cross, I've got some important decisions to make. Am I going to continue to serve Caiaphas who killed this good man? Or am I going to live to serve this good man who did nothing to Caiaphas? This healed ear on the side of my head, though it can't say a word, is speaking volumes to me, here beneath the cross of the One who healed it.

Malchus' thoughts beneath the Cross:
Beneath the Cross of Jesus, my thoughts are forced above
For in His holy humble gaze, I see His perfect love
E'en though I've hurt Him many ways, He is His Father's Son
And now beneath His cross I see, He is the Holy One.

Verse 2 Beneath the Cross of Jesus

What do you hear tonight from the One who healed you? Can you hear His love? His compassion? His desire to heal you through His many wounds?

So also, even in His dying there that Good Friday possibly stood another disciple, the one Jesus nicknamed, the Rock, the man named Simon Peter:

Peter:_____

I can't believe I let Him down! I can't believe I denied even knowing Him! Here was my chance to be true to death and I blew it. And after He warned me of exactly that just an hour before in the upper room. "No," I said, "Although all the others desert You, I never will!" I boasted. "I will stand by You no matter what."

"Before the rooster crows tomorrow morning, you will deny that you know me three times," he said. And just like that I did.

He told me I was a rock. Hardly. More like jello. In the courtyard of the high priest last night as I warmed myself by his fire, one of the servant girls told the others she had seen me with Jesus but I lied and said I wasn't. Then another said the same thing but I lied again. Then someone else at the fire recognized my Galilean accent and connected the dots, but still I lied, even calling down curses on myself. And just then, that rooster crowed.

As soon as it did, Jesus glanced through the crowd and our eyes met. I've been crying ever since. How could I have done that? And now He's hanging there on the cross just one breath away from death. Neither I nor anyone else can do anything to stop it. The very least I could do was to stand with Him. I will regret my actions the rest of my life. If only I could tell Him I'm sorry. If only I had another chance. If only I could get a do over.

I started following Him up in Galilee nearly three years ago. He called my brother Andrew and I to follow Him after He'd just helped us catch the most fish we'd ever caught. And we did. As time went by, we began to see and respect His power. We saw Him heal the sick, feed the hungry, give sight to the blind, walk on the water and even raise the dead. No one had ever done such things before. He had to be from God. And when He asked me point blank who I thought He was, I told Him, You are the Christ, the Son of the Living God. He didn't deny it, in fact He affirmed it. So why did I do what I did? Having known Him so well, how could I possibly say I didn't know Him?

If I could only get a do over. If I could only tell Him how sorry I am and do something for this Man who has done so much for me. The man whose cross I stand here beneath.

Beneath the Cross of Jesus: Verse 4

At least one other person was very aware of the crucifixion and probably witnessed it first hand. His name was Joseph and was from the town of Arimathea. He was not related to Jesus nor had he followed Him as a disciple, but it's obvious that God was at work in his heart. Listen in on his thoughts.

Joseph of Arimathea _____

As a member of the Jewish ruling council, I was one of only a small few who argued for Jesus' fair treatment. Even though most of the others were dead set against Him, I wanted to at least give Him an honest hearing. I didn't know whether He was who He said He was or not, but I had heard many reports of incredible healings and other miracles He had done. As they say in business, it's hard to argue with success.

Nevertheless, the other council members were determined to either shut this man up or kill him. It looks like they've now done both.

Growing up in a strict Jewish home, I had memorized the Holy Scriptures and knew that the prophets had foretold the coming of a Messiah. While I didn't understand exactly when or how this person would come, I anxiously awaited His arrival and prayed for it every single day. I kept my eyes and ears open to any possibilities and weighed the words and actions of many self-proclaimed saviors with those of the prophets. None of them measured up. Each one either contradicted the prophecies or failed to live up to the Law.

At least until Jesus. I couldn't get around His teachings, His parables, and His love. Whenever He spoke, He had such love in His eyes for the common people who flocked to hear Him. The priests and the Levites all seem cold and callous to the people, but not Jesus. His words and actions always reflected a heart full of compassion for these poor oppressed people who were suffering so badly.

Nicodemus shared my sympathies. He told me privately of secret conversations he'd had with Jesus and how he was convinced Jesus was someone very different. He was convinced He was from God although neither of us knew exactly what to do with Him. It was dangerous for a member of our council to get too close to such a controversial figure.

When they called the special court last night, even then He didn't respond to the high priest or to us with anger. That love that characterized His every move streamed from His eyes as He looked around the room at each of us. It was still there. I thought surely the others would see it, surely they would sense and feel it, but apparently they didn't. The armor of hatred they had built up prevented any of His love from penetrating their hearts.

When the motion was eventually made to hand Him over to Pilate for crucifixion, I objected as strongly as I could. Nicodemus stood with me, but all the others disagreed. We were completely overruled, ignored, and even ridiculed.

Many of my colleagues believe that unless the teaching comes from the priests at the temple, it is no good. They discount and dismiss every other preacher without even hearing what he has to say. I've been more open noticing that throughout the Old Testament, God often brought prophets in from outside the established order to speak truth to those in power. Many of the outsiders are crackpots to be sure, but give each one a fair hearing.

This I did with John. John the Baptizer, they called him. He was a wild one, living out in the dessert and eating locusts and wild honey. He dressed very odd too but His words were convicting and powerful. It's no wonder people went to him in droves to listen and to be baptized. Although I attended many of his services, I resisted his baptism as I knew it wouldn't be well received by the other council members.

One day while I was watching John baptize many, this Jesus came forward and John baptized him. It was amazing. After he did so, something like a dove came down and rested on Jesus and we all heard something like a voice from heaven. After that day, John kept pointing his followers in Jesus' direction. "He must become greater, I must become less," John kept saying.

So I listened to Jesus. His words made a lot of sense and His love was hard to resist. And now I can't believe that we've killed Him. I say we, because even though I tried to stop it, I am still a member of the Sanhedrin and as such am responsible for its actions. After last night and today, I may resign. I've worked all my life to get to this position of power and influence, but some things just aren't worth it. Killing One who claimed to be the Son of God and very well might have been is surely one of them.

I don't know what the consequences might be, but I'm going to give this man a decent burial. For doing so they may kick me out, and I actually hope they do, but I've got to do what God is moving me to do. I just bought a new tomb right near here and I'll gladly give permanent shelter to the remains of this Holy Man. It's the least I can do.

I will go and ask Pilate for His body, and then Nicodemus and I will lay it in my tomb. We won't have time before sundown for all the proper preparations, but we can come back on Sunday to finish up. At any rate, I've got to get moving for this Man, this God, deserves a proper burial.

Beneath the Cross of Jesus; Verse 1

And so Joseph of Arimathea did exactly that. And after the centurion assured Pilate that Jesus was in fact dead, Joseph and his friend on the council, Nicodemus, wrapped Jesus in some spices and linen and laid Jesus' body on the cold stone slab, rolled a stone in front of the entrance, and headed home to observe the Sabbath. And there we will leave him until Sunday morning.

But as we linger here beneath the cross of Jesus tonight, what's going through your mind? What's going through your heart? Pause a few moments now and meditate, contemplate, and pray. Consider which of the individuals beneath that cross you relate most with: John, Caiaphas, Peter, Mary, Malchus, Barabbas, Mary Magdalene, or Joseph of Arimathea. Perhaps some of all 8. Tell God what's on your heart as you pause here silently beneath the cross of Jesus.

Silent Prayer
Spoken prayer led by narrator.

Beneath the Cross of Jesus: Verses 1 and 4

As we go out tonight, pick up cross out of the basket. Keep it with you at least till Sunday morning to remind you of what happened on it so many years ago today. Remember and worship and thank Him.

Suggestion for Easter Sunday: Perhaps a reflection from a Roman Guard that was at the crucifixion and who passed out guarding Jesus' Tomb.

Isaiah and Jesus

(Originally celebrated at Antioch Church of the Brethren on Good Friday 2015)

This Good Friday service helps participants experience
how Isaiah's prophecy was so perfectly fulfilled
by Jesus' arrest, trial, and crucifixion.

As we come to this service tonight, I invite you to do so quietly and reverently. Of all the services we have, this is one of our most sober and reflective for tonight we especially memorialize our Savior's suffering for each of us. Please be sure your cell phones are off.

And let's take some time to turn off our to-do list as well. Lay down the pressures of this day to contemplate your Savior for the next hour.

Silent prayer.

Father we have come away for this time tonight to honor the suffering and death of your Son. We lay aside the cares of this day and the burdens of our being, knowing that you are in charge of each one. Guard our hearts and minds during this time and enable us to enter into the experience of long ago. For it's in Jesus' Name we pray, Amen.

Let us turn in our hymnals to Hymn _____ Near the Cross and just remain seated as we sing. This hymn is not a hymn of praise, but rather a quiet prayer of petition. As you sing it tonight, truly pray and ask Jesus to keep you near the cross during our time together this evening to experience the sacrifice of our Lord .

Hymn Near the Cross

The statement has been attributed to J. Vernon Magee, but he seems to indicate another has said it. Regardless of who uttered it, it's truth is the same, "Prophecy is the mold into which history is poured."

The Bible tells us that God is the Alpha and the Omega and knows the Beginning and the End and all things in between. As it seems good to Him, God will sometimes reveal to His servants, the prophets, various events that will take place in the future.

The earliest prophecy took place in the Garden of Eden when God Himself promised that Eve's Seed would eventually rise up to crush the Serpent's head. Later God told Noah of the approaching flood and Abraham of his future offspring. God revealed future events to Daniel, Ezekiel, Samuel, Jeremiah and many others in the Old Testament as well as to Paul and John in the New.

There is one prophecy, however, that we want to pay particular attention to tonight. It is the one from Isaiah 53 which is oftentimes referred to as the passage of the

Suffering Servant. Nowhere in all the Bible is such a clear portrait painted, nor such a detailed mold prepared for Jesus' crucifixion and death. As we listen to the prophet's words tonight, keep in mind that this prophecy came over 700 years before Jesus was even born.

To help us meditate on Jesus' final hours we will read this prophecy line by line and see it's perfect fulfillment primarily in John's gospel, though we will glance at a few others as well. We will be using the Old Testament to help us understand the New and vice versa, for both make up one unbroken story of Jesus Christ.

Let us begin as we hear now the words of Isaiah 53:1

Who has believed our message and to whom has the arm of the Lord been revealed?

Isaiah throws out a question to see if anyone is listening. Is anyone paying attention? Is anyone believing? Say, "Do you believe?"

John answers that question in 1:10-11
10 He was in the world, and though the world was made through him, the world did not recognize him. 11 He came to that which was his own, but his own did not receive him.

Later, after raising Lazarus from the dead, John records, (John 12:37) Even after Jesus had done all these miraculous signs in their presence, they still would not believe in him.

And Jesus Himself answered Isaiah on His way from the Upper Room to the Garden in John 15:18-25
18 "If the world hates you, keep in mind that it hated me first. 19 If you belonged to the world, it would love you as its own. As it is, you do not belong to the world, but I have chosen you out of the world. That is why the world hates you. 20 Remember the words I spoke to you: 'No servant is greater than his master.' If they persecuted me, they will persecute you also. If they obeyed my teaching, they will obey yours also. 21 They will treat you this way because of my name, for they do not know the One who sent me. 22 If I had not come and spoken to them, they would not be guilty of sin. Now, however, they have no excuse for their sin. 23 He who hates me hates my Father as well. 24 If I had not done among them what no one else did, they would not be guilty of sin. But now they have seen these miracles, and yet they have hated both me and my Father. 25 But this is to fulfill what is written in their Law: 'They hated me without reason.'

Oh yes, Isaiah, some are listening, but not many. Not most. Most of the world has chosen to turn to another channel and tune to another station. Instead of looking to the one who gives them their very life, they have chosen entertainment instead. Don't confuse us with the facts, let us live on in our ignorant bliss laughing at a thousand sitcoms, thrilling over a thousand touchdowns, and being distracted by a thousand hobbies. Tonight as we pause to remember the suffering of our Savior, most of the world pays no mind. Most of the people God created in His image are out using the very energy and life He has granted them to run away from Him. And even worse, to hate Him. Jesus promised His followers that most would not listen to their message and that the world would hate us because they hated Him first. Unfortunately, the answer to Isaiah's question is that most aren't listening or paying attention or believing. But to some, the Lord's arm has been revealed. Some have believed His message and some of them have come to remember tonight.

Isaiah declares in verse 2 that He grew up like a tender shoot, and like a root out of dry ground.

Say "tender shoot."

In the midst of the Judean countryside, Jesus sprang up. Other than His cousin, John the Baptist, Jesus appeared in a prophet's desert. Since Malachi 400 years earlier, no prophet had appeared. Even though the synagogues were open they had a form of godliness but denied His power. And into this barrenness, out of this dry ground, Jesus, the righteous shoot of David, the holy branch sprang up to grow. Like a daffodil emerging from the winter barrenness carrying with it the promise of life and beauty. After His Last Supper, Jesus put it this way,

John 15:1-8 "I am the true vine, and my Father is the gardener. 2 He cuts off every branch in me that bears no fruit, while every branch that does bear fruit he prunes so that it will be even more fruitful. 3 You are already clean because of the word I have spoken to you. 4 Remain in me, and I will remain in you. No branch can bear fruit by itself; it must remain in the vine. Neither can you bear fruit unless you remain in me.
5 "I am the vine; you are the branches. If a man remains in me and I in him, he will bear much fruit; apart from me you can do nothing. 6 If anyone does not remain in me, he is like a branch that is thrown away and withers; such branches are picked up, thrown into the fire and burned. 7 If you remain in me and my words remain in you, ask whatever you wish, and it will be given you. 8 This is to my Father's glory, that you bear much fruit, showing yourselves to be my disciples.

Indeed, the Tender Branch has grown up out of parched ground and has invited us to be grafted into Himself. To be joined to Him. We can be a part of His vine. He can empower us to bear much fruit for Him. Behold the Tender Shoot sprouting forth.

Isaiah states: He had no beauty or majesty to attract us to him, nothing in his appearance that we should desire him.

Say "No beauty."
Indeed, it appears that Jesus did not have the handsomeness of David, nor the visible strength of Sampson. He did not have the flowing hair of Absalom nor the ornamented robes of Solomon. By all accounts, He was rather plain in appearance, rather ordinary. Little did we know the majesty and beauty that lay under His tanned Middle Eastern skin.

After healing the man born blind, John tells us (John 9:28-29) Then they hurled insults at him and said, "You are this fellow's disciple! We are disciples of Moses! 29 We know that God spoke to Moses, but as for this fellow, we don't even know where he comes from."

There was nothing in His earthly appearance to attract others or make us desire Him. So we didn't. Looking back, however, Paul saw and called our attention to His majesty and beauty in Philippians 2:5-8
5 Your attitude should be the same as that of Christ Jesus: 6 Who, being in very nature God, did not consider equality with God something to be grasped, 7 but made himself nothing, taking the very nature of a servant, being made in human likeness. 8 And being found in appearance as a man, he humbled himself and became obedient to death — even death on a cross!

Indeed. Jesus laid aside His heavenly robes and eternal majesty to take on the robe of flesh. To perspire and smell like a human, to appear as an ordinary person. To be one of us. With no apparent beauty or majesty. In fact, by the time all was said and done, Isaiah 52:14 tells us that His appearance was so disfigured beyond that of any man and his form marred beyond human likeness.

And Isaiah tells us that this ordinary person was despised and rejected by men,

Say "despised and rejected."
John tells us how He was indeed despised and rejected during His trial before

Pilate, (19:4-7) 4 Once more Pilate came out and said to the Jews, "Look, I am bringing him out to you to let you know that I find no basis for a charge against him." 5 When Jesus came out wearing the crown of thorns and the purple robe, Pilate said to them, "Here is the man!"
6 As soon as the chief priests and their officials saw him, they shouted, "Crucify! Crucify!"
But Pilate answered, "You take him and crucify him. As for me, I find no basis for a charge against him."
7 The Jews insisted, "We have a law, and according to that law he must die, because he claimed to be the Son of God."

The One who loved all was despised by most. Not just disliked, but despised. Hated. Rejected. How the Jewish leaders loved to hate this Man. They despised Him so much that they preferred a murderer over Him and they rejected Him so much they called for His crucifixion. And if that weren't enough, Matthew tells us that as He hung on the cross,
(Matt 27:39-43) 39 Those who passed by hurled insults at him, shaking their heads 40 and saying, "You who are going to destroy the temple and build it in three days, save yourself! Come down from the cross, if you are the Son of God!"
41 In the same way the chief priests, the teachers of the law and the elders mocked him. 42 "He saved others," they said, "but he can't save himself! He's the King of Israel! Let him come down now from the cross, and we will believe in him. 43 He trusts in God. Let God rescue him now if he wants him, for he said, 'I am the Son of God.'"

Behold Jesus, our Creator and Sustainer, our Lover and Savior, Despised and rejected.
During the instrumental, consider how Jesus was despised and rejected and consider how He continues to be despised and rejected today.

Instrumental

Isaiah tells us He was a man of sorrows.

Everyone say "sorrows."
In John 11, we see Him heavy with sorrow at the tomb of His dear friend Lazarus.
33 When Jesus saw her weeping, and the Jews who had come along with her also weeping, he was deeply moved in spirit and troubled. 34 "Where have you laid him?" he asked.

"Come and see, Lord," they replied.
35 Jesus wept.
36 Then the Jews said, "See how he loved him!"

Later, in the Garden, His sorrow has reached the breaking point

Matt 26:36-39 36 Then Jesus went with his disciples to a place called Gethsemane, and he said to them, "Sit here while I go over there and pray." 37 He took Peter and the two sons of Zebedee along with him, and he began to be **sorrowful** and troubled. 38 Then he said to them, "My soul is overwhelmed with **sorrow** to the point of death. Stay here and keep watch with me." 39 Going a little farther, he fell with his face to the ground and prayed, "My Father, if it is possible, may this cup be taken from me. Yet not as I will, but as you will."

Jesus knew what sorrow was all about. He had His share of sadness and heartbreak. He wept with those who wept and mourned with those who mourned. And He had His own heartbreaks as well. He was a man of sorrows

Poem: Man of Sorrows

Man of sorrows what a name
for the Son of God, who came
ruined sinners to reclaim:
Hallelujah, what a Savior!

Isaiah also says He was familiar with suffering.

Say "Suffering"
Indeed, that He was. For He suffered in the Garden:

Luke 22:41-44 He withdrew about a stone's throw beyond them, knelt down and prayed, 42 "Father, if you are willing, take this cup from me; yet not my will, but yours be done." 43 An angel from heaven appeared to him and strengthened him. 44 And being in anguish, he prayed more earnestly, and his sweat was like drops of blood falling to the ground.

Besides the Garden, He suffered at the hands of the guards and the soldiers. And He suffered unbelievable agony and pain on the cross. He suffered physically as He endured the whips and thorns and nails, and He suffered spiritually as the weight of the world's billions of sinners weighed upon Him. He suffered for every abused wife and every neglected child. He suffered for every betrayed man and every murder victim. He suffered for every time the Ten Commandments have ever been broken and for every time we failed to love God with all our hearts, souls, minds, and strength or failed to love our neighbors as ourselves. He suffered for every prodigal spirit and action. Every adultery and every fornication. For all the pornography and drunkenness, for all our racism and violence and rebellion. Familiar with suffering? Very much so. Much more familiar with it than we will ever be.

Isaiah tells us He is, "Like one from whom men hide their faces he was despised, and we esteemed him not."

Say "We esteemed Him not."
John says, (19:14-15) It was the day of Preparation of Passover Week, about the sixth hour. "Here is your king," Pilate said to the Jews.
15 But they shouted, "Take him away! Take him away! Crucify him!"
"Shall I crucify your king?" Pilate asked.
"We have no king but Caesar," the chief priests answered.

We esteemed Him not. We valued Him not. Instead of seeing Him as the priceless gem that He was, we saw only a worthless rock. Only dirt and gravel. Instead of recognizing Him and esteeming Him as the King of the Universe, we despised Him and turned our faces away. Oh God, forgive us for failing to give Jesus the proper esteem even today that He so rightly deserves. Help us to recognize His proper value and accord to Him the honor that goes with it. Ask God to help you do that now during this instrumental.

Instrumental for Reflection.

Isaiah tells us that, "Surely he took up our infirmities and carried our sorrows,"

Say "He took up ours."
John tells us (19:16-18) Finally Pilate handed him over to them to be crucified. So the soldiers took charge of Jesus. 17 Carrying his own cross, he went out to the place of the Skull (which in Aramaic is called Golgotha).

When Jesus took up that cross, He took up our infirmities. When He hoisted it onto His holy shoulder, he carried our sorrows. And even though Simon was drafted into helping carry the cross, Jesus, and Jesus alone continued to carry our sorrows and infirmities up Calvary's Hill.

Poem: Blessed Redeemer
Up Calvary's mountain, one dreadful morn,
Walked Christ my Savior, weary and worn;
Facing for sinners death on the cross,
That He might save us from endless loss.

"Father forgive them!" thus did He pray,
E'en while His lifeblood flowed fast away;
Praying for sinners while in such woe
No one but Jesus ever loved so.

Blessèd Redeemer! Precious Redeemer!
Seems now I see Him on Calvary's tree;
Wounded and bleeding, for sinners pleading,
Blind and unheeding—dying for me!

Isaiah says, "yet we considered him stricken by God, smitten by him, and afflicted."

Say "stricken by God."
John says, (19:7-12) 7 The Jews insisted, "We have a law, and according to that law he must die, because he claimed to be the Son of God."
8 When Pilate heard this, he was even more afraid, 9 and he went back inside the palace. "Where do you come from?" he asked Jesus, but Jesus gave him no answer. 10 "Do you refuse to speak to me?" Pilate said. "Don't you realize I have power either to free you or to crucify you?"
11 Jesus answered, "You would have no power over me if it were not given to you from above. Therefore the one who handed me over to you is guilty of a greater sin."
12 From then on, Pilate tried to set Jesus free, but the Jews kept shouting, "If you let this man go, you are no friend of Caesar. Anyone who claims to be a king opposes Caesar."

Somehow we mistook **our** cruelty for that of God. We thought God was bringing to Him just punishment and affliction. Little did we know how wrong we had it. **We were smiting Him. We were afflicting Him. We were striking Him. Not God.** Let us be very careful before we assume what does and what does not come from God.

Isaiah says, "But he was pierced for our transgressions,"

Say "pierced for my transgressions."

John says, (19:31-35) 31 Now it was the day of Preparation, and the next day was to be a special Sabbath. Because the Jews did not want the bodies left on the crosses during the Sabbath, they asked Pilate to have the legs broken and the bodies taken down. 32 The soldiers therefore came and broke the legs of the first man who had been crucified with Jesus, and then those of the other. 33 But when they came to Jesus and found that he was already dead, they did not break his legs. 34 Instead, one of the soldiers pierced Jesus' side with a spear, bringing a sudden flow of blood and water.

To be pierced is very painful. It is an open and direct violation of our skin and the muscles and organs inside. And Jesus was pierced. Prior to His piercing by the sword, which He did not feel since He was already dead, He had already been pierced by nails which He did feel. Nails that crunched through skin, tissue and bone to affix this innocent man to our cross.

The nails that pierced Him were not for anything He had done, but rather for what you and I have done. Because we lust, He was pierced. Because we hate and covet and cuss, the nails pierced His holy hands. Because of our greed and gossip and pride, His holy feet were driven through. Because we lie, He had to die. He was pierced for our transgressions.

Bearing shame and scoffing rude,
in my place condemned he stood,
sealed my pardon with his blood:
Hallelujah, what a Savior!

As we consider the pierced side of our Savior, let us sing together hymn ____, There Is a Fountain

Isaiah says, "He was crushed for our iniquities; the punishment that brought us peace was upon him, and by his wounds we are healed."

Say "By His wounds we are healed."

John says, (19:1-3) 1 Then Pilate took Jesus and had him flogged. 2 The soldiers twisted together a crown of thorns and put it on his head. They clothed him in a purple robe 3 and went up to him again and again, saying, "Hail, king of the Jews!" And they struck him in the face.

Jesus was crushed for our iniquities. His body was crushed. His Spirit was crushed. His heart was crushed. For us. For our failure to trust and insistence on worry. For our gluttony and laziness. For our grumbling and complaining. For our thanklessness and selfishness, Jesus was crushed.

We might tonight think of a giant vice clamping shut on Him. Even though not one of His bones was broken, His heart certainly was. The punishment that He received has purchased peace for us. The wounds from the flogging and thorns, the black eyes and the swollen face, He endured all of it so that we could be healed. So that the giant oozing gangrene gash of sin in our soul could be healed back to health and mended to wholeness.

Paul says it very well in 2 Cor 5: 21 where He says, "God made him who had no sin to be sin for us, so that in him we might become the righteousness of God."

His punishment brought us peace. His wounds healed our sin.

Play Song "I Walked Today Where Jesus Walked."

But Isaiah reminds us, "We all, like sheep, have gone astray, each of us has turned to his own way; and the Lord has laid on him the iniquity of us all."

Say "I've gone astray."

Indeed, when Jesus was enduring His worst, the disciples each turned to His own way. Matthew says that "all the disciples deserted Him and fled." (Matt 26:56)
While John says (John 18:15-27)
15 Simon Peter and another disciple were following Jesus. Because this disciple was known to the high priest, he went with Jesus into the high priest's courtyard, 16 but Peter had to wait outside at the door. The other disciple, who was known to the high priest, came back, spoke to the girl on duty there and brought Peter in.
17 "You are not one of his disciples, are you?" the girl at the door asked Peter.
He replied, "I am not."
18 It was cold, and the servants and officials stood around a fire they had made to keep warm. Peter also was standing with them, warming himself.

25 As Simon Peter stood warming himself, he was asked, "You are not one of his disciples, are you?"
He denied it, saying, "I am not."
26 One of the high priest's servants, a relative of the man whose ear Peter had cut off, challenged him, "Didn't I see you with him in the olive grove?" 27 Again Peter denied it, and at that moment a rooster began to crow.

How prone we are to go our own way. To turn away, especially at the first sign of pain trouble or hardship. We'd like to think we wouldn't do what the disciples did that night and yet we likely did so just today when we were too ashamed to mention Jesus to a coworker. When we were too embarrassed to invite our neighbor. When we turned away ourselves and did that which we knew to be wrong. We all like sheep have turned away, each of us has gone our own way. Everyone say "Baaa" We are all sheep.

Isaiah proclaims, "He was oppressed and afflicted, yet he did not open his mouth; he was led like a lamb to the slaughter, and as a sheep before her shearers is silent, so he did not open his mouth."

Say "He was silent."
John tells us (19:7-9) The Jews insisted, "We have a law, and according to that law he must die, because he claimed to be the Son of God."
8 When Pilate heard this, he was even more afraid, 9 and he went back inside the palace. "Where do you come from?" he asked Jesus, but Jesus gave him no answer.

Though Jesus could have destroyed His accusers with the breath of His mouth, He said not a word. He willingly allowed them to lead Him, the condemned Lamb of God, to His sacrificial death. Though He could have defended Himself better than any Hollywood lawyer, He stood silent and let them slaughter Him. As silently as a sheep is before her shearers.

Guilty, helpless, lost were we;
blameless Lamb of God was he,
sacrificed to set us free:
Hallelujah, what a Savior!

Isaiah asks, "By oppression and judgment he was taken away. And who can speak of his descendants? For he was cut off from the land of the living; for the transgression of my people he was stricken."

Say "cut off."

John speaks of His cut off from the land of the living (19:28-30)

28 Later, knowing that all was now completed, and so that the Scripture would be fulfilled, Jesus said, "I am thirsty." 29 A jar of wine vinegar was there, so they soaked a sponge in it, put the sponge on a stalk of the hyssop plant, and lifted it to Jesus' lips. 30 When he had received the drink, Jesus said, "It is finished." With that, he bowed his head and gave up his spirit.

The Shoot that had grown out of dry ground was now cut off. It was severed in the prime of His life. It was chopped down and destroyed without mercy. The daffodil was mowed off by a weedeater. The life of our Lord was brutally cut off from the land of the living.

He was lifted up to die;
"It is finished" was his cry;
now in heaven exalted high:
Hallelujah, what a Savior!

Let us sing together, hymn _____ Song- When I Survey

Isaiah goes on to tell us that after His death, "He was assigned a grave with the wicked, and with the rich in his death, though he had done no violence, nor was any deceit in his mouth."

Say "buried with the rich."

No part of prophecy's mold would be unfilled. No detail was left to fall to the ground. No facet of the blueprint was left uncompleted.

John is very clear about where Jesus' grave was assigned (in 19:38-42)

38 Later, Joseph of Arimathea asked Pilate for the body of Jesus. Now Joseph was a disciple of Jesus, but secretly because he feared the Jews. With Pilate's permission, he came and took the body away. 39 He was accompanied by Nicodemus, the man who earlier had visited Jesus at night. Nicodemus brought a mixture of myrrh and aloes, about seventy-five pounds. 40 Taking Jesus' body, the two of them wrapped it, with the spices, in strips of linen. This was in accordance with Jewish burial customs. 41 At the place where Jesus was crucified, there was a garden, and in the garden a new tomb, in which no one had ever been laid. 42 Because it was the Jewish day of Preparation and since the tomb was nearby, they laid Jesus there.

We know today that in order to afford such a tomb, Joseph of Arimathea was obviously a wealthy man. Out of His decency and respect for Jesus, he and Nicodemus performed what they thought would be their last act of respect for what they saw as the dead prophet.

Isaiah finishes His prophecy by declaring,
10 Yet it was the Lord's will to crush him and cause him to suffer, and though the Lord makes his life a guilt offering, he will see his offspring and prolong his days, and the will of the Lord will prosper in his hand. 11 After the suffering of his soul, he will see the light [of life] and be satisfied; by his knowledge my righteous servant will justify many, and he will bear their iniquities. 12 Therefore I will give him a portion among the great, and he will divide the spoils with the strong, because he poured out his life unto death, and was numbered with the transgressors. For he bore the sin of many, and made intercession for the transgressors.

Say "numbered with the transgressors."

Jesus was not crucified alone as we read from John earlier, (John 19:18) Here they crucified him, and with him two others — one on each side and Jesus in the middle.

Luke goes into a little more detail about the transgressors with whom Jesus was numbered. Listen to his account (Luke 23:32-43)
32 Two other men, both criminals, were also led out with him to be executed. 33 When they came to the place called the Skull, there they crucified him, along with the criminals — one on his right, the other on his left. 34 Jesus said, "Father, forgive them, for they do not know what they are doing." And they divided up his clothes by casting lots.
39 One of the criminals who hung there hurled insults at him: "Aren't you the Christ? Save yourself and us!"
40 But the other criminal rebuked him. "Don't you fear God," he said, "since you are under the same sentence? 41 We are punished justly, for we are getting what our deeds deserve. But this man has done nothing wrong."
42 Then he said, "Jesus, remember me when you come into your kingdom."
43 Jesus answered him, "I tell you the truth, today you will be with me in paradise."

Even in His great humiliation and death, Jesus continued to exude love and forgiveness. Exactly as Isaiah prophesied, Jesus not only bore the sin of many there upon the cross that day but He clearly made intercession for the transgressors with whom He died. Not only did He grant eternal life to His partner in death, but just a little while before He prayed forgiveness for the very ones who were nailing Him to the cross. Such peace and love are hard to comprehend.

The most amazing part of all of this is that Isaiah also saw beyond the crucifixion to the Resurrection when He talked about how God would prolong His days and enable Him to see the light of life, but we'll save that for Sunday morning. It is enough tonight to see the suffering of our Savior fulfilling every last detail in the mold of Isaiah's ancient prophecy. And as we've seen it again, to pause and consider the great price that was paid for our sins. The great price that Jesus paid that we might be saved, and to spend eternity with Him.

When he comes, our glorious King,
all his ransomed home to bring,
then anew this song we'll sing:
Hallelujah, what a Savior!

Take a few moments now during the instrumental to meditate and thank Jesus for the Price He paid to purchase your soul.

Instrumental

As we honor Jesus' great sacrifice for us, let us join our voices in singing, Beneath The Cross of Jesus. Number _____

We will go out tonight leaving Jesus in the borrowed tomb of Joseph, and looking forward to a surprise and celebration on Sunday morning.

Closing Prayer

Suggestion for Easter Sunday: Highlight how Jesus' Resurrection fulfills Isaiah's prophecies in Isaiah 53:10-12.

Afterword

My prayer is that these Good Friday Services have been a blessing to you personally and to the congregation to which you minister. Thank you for your faithfulness to Jesus and to His Church and may God bless you richly as you continue to serve Him.

Finally, my Brethren, be strong in the Lord, and in the power of His might. Peace be to the Brethren, and love with faith, from God the Father and the Lord Jesus Christ. Grace be with all them that love our Lord Jesus Christ in sincerity. Amen.

Ephesians 6:10, 23-24

Other Books By
George A. Bowers, Sr.

  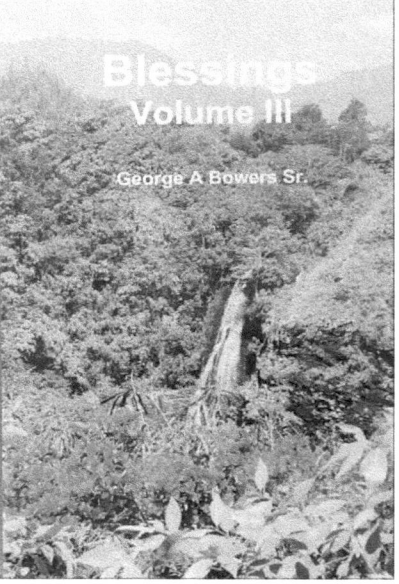

Blessings and Blessings Volumes II and III are devotional books with rich collections of modern parables for each week of the year.

Celebration Time includes several Brethren Love Feasts featuring various themes.

From The Horse's Mouth contains 17 first person vignettes from Biblical characters.

Faithful Footsteps includes 32 devotions with poems on The Holy Land.

Wit and Wisdom Of The Woods has many poems about hunting and the outdoors.

Brethren Verses includes poems related to Brethren history & heritage.

Holy Land Verses is a collection of poems about Israel.

Personal Verses is a collection of poems about many Bible characters.

Holy Verses features poems about Holy Week, Good Friday and Easter.

Valley Verses and
Valley Verses Volumes II, III, IV, V, VI
and VII are collections of poems arranged
according to various topics such
as Nature, Holidays, Humor,
Biblical characters and more.

Check out www.georgebowersministries.com for
blogs and latest books and resources!
Follow me on Facebook!

www.ingramcontent.com/pod-product-compliance
Ingram Content Group UK Ltd.
Pitfield, Milton Keynes, MK11 3LW, UK
UKHW051520230225
4720UKWH00023B/214